SUPERIOR CUSTOMER EXPERIENCE

The New Business Brand

WILLIS AMACH

Hezma Ventures

ISBN-13: 978-9966-8275-4-8

Cover design and layout done by Hezma Ventures, Bungoma Kenya

Printed in Kenya

Unless indicated otherwise, all Quotes used in this book have been taken
from the Brainy Quotes website https://www.brainyquote.com

DEDICATION

*To all the great men and women who have dedicated themselves
to the pursuit of excellence and offering superior customer
experience; the world is a better place because of your
selflessness and dedication to serving humanity. This book is
dedicated to you.*

*And to all those individuals zealous to make a positive difference
in their various spheres of influence by your little contributions,
in uplifting the human spirit and inculcating the culture of
excellence in the business world today.*

*Let this jewel spur you on in your journey to greatness
and to a life of impact in this generation and leaving
a legacy for the generations to come.*

CONTENTS

FOREWORD

Offering superior customer service has been my passion for as long as I can remember. I am a firm believer in the centrality and inalienability of service excellence in the process of building of the super brands. Offering superior customer service brings untold satisfaction and enjoyment in the work when you can see that your customers are both satisfied and delighted with your services, not to mention the pleasant ripple effect of always having a steady growing stream of new customers referred to you by your evangelical customers, thus saving you lots of money in expensive marketing.

Even more importantly, superior customer service is the only business parameter that cannot be easily copied by the competition. Superior service offering sets a brand apart and puts it in its own league, away from the sea of business entities whose primary preoccupation is to either compete on prices of the increasingly commoditized products and services or to cooperate like cartels on the same.

It therefore gives me great pleasure to be a partaker in this classic work that has been done to empower entrepreneurs, employees and management teams of business entities and other organizations on this timeless subject of superior customer experience. The book spells out in both relatable and useful way all matters of service excellence; and the information contained herein can be used by any individual or corporation to turn around their business and personal fortunes.

This book that has been written by another customer service aficionado is a gem that will bring you great returns for many years to come. Grab it, read it, and brainstorm on the ideas presented herein with your teams; but even more importantly put into practice the wisdom gleaned from its pages thereof, and watch your business enterprise or organization turn around for the better.

I have personally known Willis for more than a decade now and I can vouch for his passion and consistency in delivering superior customer experience to his customers on the one hand, and ensuring that the same ideal of service excellence is practiced by all who work with him on the other hand. Willis is therefore a true embodiment of what he preaches.

Superior customer experience is indeed the new business brand; this is the new game changer in these times that are characterized by cutthroat competition, with commoditized products and services, not to mention the ever increasing government oversight on business practices. This new business environment has given birth to new breed of customers that are both increasingly informed and spoilt for choices. However, when you make service excellence the defining attribute of your business operations, you have no reason to be alarmed by all these ground realities; your evangelical customers will both love you and grow your brand for you.

Grab this opportunity and embark on the rewarding journey of offering service excellence to your customers and join the elite club of the super achievers. Your customers are waiting.

Albina Ochembo
Senior Manager—Customer Experience, Equity Group Holdings

PREFACE

The business environment has witnessed so many defining changes over the last two decades. Many givens of yesteryears are no longer guaranteed. Old business rules have been shattered and in their place, radical changes have become the new normal. The market has witnessed massive economic slowdown caused by a combination of several factors such as credit crunches, asset bubbles, high interest rates and widespread loss of confidence in investment and the economy by the middle class, among others. ***This has resulted into slower business growth.***

All the business sectors are experiencing relative levels of turbulence with some new emerging risks that were hitherto unknown, brought about by both globalization and technological advancement. Risk management therefore has taken on a new meaning and has become a major function of every role in the business leadership. Various governments have also taken on new roles in the economies of their jurisdictions—some have come in as business allies while others have come in as adversaries; furthermore, the regulators have sharply focused their lenses on the risk mitigation function in every industry.

Most importantly, ***products and services have become increasingly commoditized.*** This widespread duplication of products and services in every industry has naturally taken the battle for customers' acquisition and retention to another level—that of ***cutthroat competition.*** Customers are not only now spoilt for choices but are much more informed than in the previous periods. In addition, competitors are now actively searching for any possible advantage in every area of product and service offering—in the use of technology, choice of prime locations, reduction in prices and giving of discounts among others.

The import of these changes has been twofold: ***the first one is the permanent disruption of the old business models*** and the ushering in of a new breed of technologically driven businesses; secondly, is ***the greater focus on the customer experience as the new frontier in the war of customer acquisition and retention.***

To thrive and succeed in business in such environment requires a paradigm shift in the business approach—this is where service excellence comes in. Granted, we all want our business ventures to become successful; we all desire to have a larger market share and more revenues from increased sales. We all would want to be the preferred go-to business for the customers when they have to make every purchase decision. We all want to leave a positive legacy by impacting lives and livelihoods for posterity. And we naturally desire to have a sustainable business growth. Interestingly everybody in the increasingly crowded market apparently wants the same things—***the only difference is how each one goes about in achieving the same.***

In such an environment of cutthroat competition, superior customer experience becomes the only time-tested and guaranteed business lifeline. ***The only differentiator of the few great companies from the mediocre majority is the personal experience that businesses are able to create in the lives of their customers.*** Certain parameters are clearly outside the control of a business entity such as the actions of the competitors and the government policies. It is both foolhardy and a waste of precious resources to focus attention and energy on such parameters. You can instead focus on what the business can truly control—***the experience of the customers with a brand.***

Whereas it is true that technology has permanently disrupted and redefined how companies interact with their customers, customers still expect that businesses will both take care of their needs and give them personalized attention.

Customers today use multiple channels and platforms to connect with a business including calls, e-mail and chat. *When they connect with a brand on any one of these channels, they expect to be known and be served on demand regardless of the channel used.* In reality, the customers want to have seamless engagement across multiple trustworthy platforms and channels. Furthermore, customers today demand products, services and experiences that are relevant and that meet their needs and wants in the moment.

Creating a memorable and powerful experience for the customers in such circumstances could seem to be complicated given the multiplicity of channels involved. This is only technically true. *The good news however, is that the customers still want the same things they have always wanted—and that is to be taken care of.* Granted, they are now more demanding, more informed and much more impatient. They expect their problems to be solved faster, since technology has put at our disposal the tools to offer such speeds. *The service provider that excels at personalizing their customers' experience without compromising quality would readily win more consumers in this war of customer acquisition and retention.*

The customers' interactions with a business at every touch point are what define the customer experience with a given brand. *The company may talk about its brand promise but ultimately it's the customers who decide whether the brand promise was delivered or not.* Everything a business does—from its market outreach, advertisement, research, sales and after-sales service, and much more—all play a significant role in shaping the customer experience.

When you get this customer experience right through the consistent provision of delightful and amazing experiences, that put a smile on the customers' faces and keep them coming back for more, then you don't have to worry about the competition. You shall have succeeded in connecting with the minds and hearts of your customers who then become your loyal fans freely broadcasting how incredible it is to do business with your brand.

Leading brands such as Amazon and Zappos are not leading by chance—it took them considerable time and consistent effort to perfect their philosophy and practice of offering service excellence. They have gone beyond engaging in transactional businesses to building on-going business relationships with their customers. As a result they have won an ever growing army of evangelical customers, increased their sales volumes and revenues, and exponentially grown their shareholder value.

Customer experience is indeed the new frontier in the war of customer acquisition and retention. This is the new business brand. This book shows you how you too can win by inculcating a culture of service excellence in your company. There is still a huge opportunity for business growth and the creation of lasting positive legacies in the business world today. *You can take the right steps to make sure that your team consistently delivers an awe-inspiring service; and the result will a shot at greatness.* Your customers are waiting.

Some reflection questions have been included at the end of each chapter to aid in your reflection and team discussion wherever applicable. Feel free to contact the author in case you might need help in any of the areas touched in this book. We shall be honored to partner with you on your journey of inculcating a powerful mindset of service excellence and superior customer experience in your organization.

The Author

CHAPTER ONE: THE CURRENT BUSINESS ENVIRONMENT

"The nature of the global business environment guarantees that no matter how hard we work to create a stable and healthy organisation, our organisation will continue to experience dramatic changes far beyond our control.

MARGARET J. WHEATLEY

Time has proven the difficulty of predicting precisely what the future holds. Disruptive changes of global magnitude have happened in the last two decades that have permanently impacted how companies conduct their businesses today. The givens of the yesteryears are no longer guaranteed and nothing is the same anymore. ***The business environment has ushered in a new normal—that of working with superior technology and at great speed.*** More and more changes are in the offing if the past is anything to go by. Every company must therefore be prepared to deal with the changes as they happen.

The import of some of these changes has been massive business losses and obliteration of the shareholder value. On a positive note, a new breed of technologically driven businesses and influential business leaders have emerged that have permanently redefined the consumer market dynamics in general and customer experience in particular. Some companies have unfortunately been unable to survive these market storms and as a result have gone under.

Let's have a look at some of these changes.

Five Things Have Defined The Current Business Environment:

The following are some of the more pronounced changes that have hugely impacted the current business environment:

     i.   *Slowed down economic growth*
    ii.   *Products and Services duplication*
   iii.   *Cutthroat competition*
    iv.   *Increased governmental control*
     v.   *Greater focus on risk management*

Slowed down economic growth

A combination of several factors including the extensive credit crunches of the year 2008 and beyond (that was triggered by heavy investment in collateralized debt obligations); asset bubble bursts orchestrated by artificial and unsustainable consumer demands; high interest rates and the widespread loss of consumer confidence in investment and the economy in general by the middle class; the over-extension of the supply chains; the over-investment in marginal businesses; razor-thin inventories and fragile business models, and more recently the US-China trade wars; have all contributed to massive economic slowdown. A number of world economies are either in recession already or are getting into recession.

The slowed economic growth has resulted in sales down turn, increasing bad debts and provisions for the same; there is also eroded purchasing power of most households, fueled by inflation and massive job losses in the market. Most economic sectors such as the real estate, tourism and hospitality, entertainment and the manufacturing sectors just to mention but a few have been hit really hard. The global pandemic of Covid-19 has only made matters worse.

This state of affairs begs the question—how do businesses navigate through this economic meltdown and still thrive and succeed? The answer lies in embracing superior customer service or service excellence as a business culture.

Products and services duplication

Secondly, products and services have become increasingly commoditized. A business can no longer compete on differentiated product features or price alone. Delivery channels have equally been duplicated by the various industry players. To stand out in this crowd, you have to endeavor to do things differently—*you have to do what cannot be readily duplicated or copied by the competition.* You have to embrace a mindset of service excellence. Researcher and technology consultant John Bessant remarked that:

> *"In a world where things are increasingly becoming commodities (especially services) the real differentiator becomes the personal experience you are able to create in the lives of your customers"*

What cannot be readily duplicated or copied is the superior customer experience your customers receive while interacting with your brand at every touch point. You therefore need to build very cordial working relationships with your customers, suppliers and employees through service excellence.

Cutthroat competition

Duplication of products and services naturally takes the battle for customers' acquisition and retention to another level—*that of cutthroat competition.* Customers are now spoilt for choices; they are equally much more informed, more demanding and much more impatient than they were in the previous periods. Competitors are also searching for any possible advantage in every area of product and service offering—in the use of technology, choice of prime locations, reduction in prices and giving of discounts among others.

Because products and services delivery channels are being duplicated by the competition with increasing levels of frequency with the passage of time, customers can now easily get similar products and services from the next door neighbor or at the click of the computer button. International players are equally increasingly targeting the African market with similar products and services, at even cheaper prices.

Expecting to retain customer loyalty based on the product quality alone is a surer route to disappointment. You can however still make your business to thrive and succeed in such a crowded market by cultivating and maintaining cordial working relationships with your current and prospective customers through service excellence. *Once you win the trust and loyalty of your customers by delighting and amazing them through continued service excellence, you do not have to be overly concerned and worried about the actions of your competitors.*

In addition, flexibility and speed in assigning and re-assigning resources will make a huge difference in the company performance, in the face of unrelenting cutthroat competition.

Increased governmental control

Another big change in the business environment is the increased government oversight role in the market. Governments have taken on new roles in the economies of their jurisdictions—some have come in as business allies while others have come as adversaries.

A number of industries and business sectors such as the banking and the petroleum sectors are operating under new regulatory environments where there are new reporting regulations and price controls respectively in some jurisdictions such as Kenya. There are also increased scrutiny and quality control checks by the various government agencies.

Besides all these domestic controls, there is a widespread move towards global regulation.

Of even greater interest to businesses is **the move by governments to shield the consumers from what is termed as *unfair and unethical* business practices.** Some governments have anchored these controls in the law through legislation by acts of parliament such as the enactment of The Consumer Protection Act, 2012 Laws of Kenya. This kind of increased oversight essentially narrows down the viable legal options that businesses can take advantage of to increase their returns. However, embracing service excellence will put you ahead of the pack and actually make the law to become your ally instead of a foe.

Greater focus on risk management

Finally, there has been a greater focus on risk management as a business priority. Globalization and technological advancement has come with new risks to the businesses. All the business sectors are experiencing relative levels of turbulence, with some new risks emerging that were hitherto unknown. Risk management therefore has taken on a new meaning and has become a major function of every role within the echelons of the business leadership.

The regulators have sharply focused their lenses on the risk mitigation function in every industry. Yet it is in this same environment where the businesses are not only expected to thrive and succeed, but to also generate acceptable returns on investment to the shareholders. This calls for proper risk assessment and mitigation by the business leadership.

The good news is that when you focus on service excellence and continuously invest in the improvement of the customer experience of your customers at every touch point, you not only plug any service gaps but invariably seal any control loopholes that quickly get noticed from your customers' interactions and feedback.

Customers are the major winners in this era of the unprecedented hi-tech inventions and innovations that have compelled the industry players to relook at their experiences, and the regulators to look out for their interests. *Simply focusing on offering service excellence will position your brand to be a big winner in its specific industry in the midst of this great tectonic shift.* Companies that invest in customer service for the sake of improving their service offering will definitely create a superior experience for their customers, and the result shall be a shot at greatness.

As we **conclude** this chapter, we note that to win and thrive in this business environment where change is the only constant, and businesses are compelled to operate with a new normal, every forward looking brand must cut a customer niche for itself by consistently providing amazing and delightful customer experiences. This will earn the brand both loyal and evangelical customers. You also stand to reap big on cost-saving on areas such as advertisement and marketing campaigns, as your loyal fan base takes over the role of freely broadcasting your business within their circles of influence. *There is nothing as powerful in marketing as having a pool of delighted and happy customers freely advocating for your brand to their friends and families by word of mouth or via the social media.*

Reflection questions:

1) How has the economic meltdown impacted your industry and organization?
2) How has the product and service duplication in your industry affected your sales turnover over the past few years? If the impact of the same has been negative, how can you counter the downturn?
3) What is the impact of the governmental interventions in your industry? How can you turn those interventions into your favor?
4) Focusing on service excellence positions a brand to win big in the face of cutthroat competition, discuss.

CHAPTER TWO: WINNING IN CUSTOMER ACQUISTION AND RETENTION

"When the customer comes first, the customer will last"

–ROBERT HALF

Everything a business does—from its market outreach, advertisement, research, sales and after-sales service, and much more—all play a significant role in shaping the customer experience. This is because the customers' interactions with a business at every touch point are what defines the customer experience with a given brand. The company may state its brand promise but ultimately it is the customers who decide whether that brand promise was delivered or not.

Technology has permanently disrupted and redefined how companies interact with their customers today by providing more avenues for the customers to connect with a business. Whereas customers can today use multiple channels and platforms such as e-mail, calls and chat to contact businesses, they still expect to be served seamlessly despite the channel they have used. In other words, *when customers connect with a business on any one of these multiple channels, they expect to be known and be served on demand regardless of the channel used.*

Creating memorable and powerful experiences for the customers in such circumstances could seem to be complicated given the multiplicity of channels involved. This is however only technically true. *The good news is that the customers still want the same things they have always wanted—and that is to be taken care of.* However, they are now more demanding, more informed and much more impatient; they do expect their problems to be solved faster, since technology has put at our disposal the tools to offer such speeds.

It is imperative that a business should invest in improving their customers' experience on their various channels and touch points by not only being available in all the various platforms that the customers may choose to use, but also in seamlessly integrating those channels by a technology known as Channel-less support (We have dedicated **Chapter Four** of this book, to discuss this concept and much more in detail). Suffice to say here that channel-less support system enables the company to merge customer interaction and data into one place.

It is important to note that *customers do not really care about the multiplicity of the channels a brand could boast of having, they only care that they can connect with a brand, the way they want to connect and whenever they want to connect.* The reality on the ground is that customers typically use the channel that is easiest and most convenient for them at any particular time. This explains why investing in improved customer experience is key in winning the war on customer acquisition and retention.

Focusing on customer experience management may be the single most important investment a business can make today in an environment of cutthroat competition. According to a research on customer experience management, done in 2018 by Aberdeen Group—the US Based market intelligence and research services company, the top three drivers for investing in customer experience management are[1]:

- *Improved customer retention*

- *Improved customer satisfaction*

- *Increased cross-selling and up-selling*

Superior customer experience is fueled by the spirit of service excellence. *Service excellence dictates that you serve and exceed the expectations of your customers by putting their interests ahead of your own; and using every interaction to create powerful and memorable impressions on the customers.* It's about inculcating and nurturing a culture that values customers as individuals beyond the immediate need to close the sales deals. The mindset of offering service excellence invariably results in improved customer satisfaction.

Service excellence breeds loyal and evangelical customers whose continued business patronage and active advocacy propels a brand to achieve sustainable super profitability. Studies have shown that loyal customers are more profitable than customer churn and that better service is a key factor in retaining your best customers.

Satisfied customers essentially become evangelical and readily refer other customers to the business brand. This is the great paradox of focusing on offering superior customer service as opposed to the immediate need to close a transaction—*more customers get referred to you by the satisfied customers, hence more transactions to close.*

Spending large sums of money on expensive marketing campaigns or having sophisticated delivery channels without offering commensurate service excellence to create satisfied and happy customers is a game of musical chairs—it is not taking you anywhere. The proven most inexpensive way to have a resounding and sustainable business success in any industry is in delivering service excellence.

Service Excellence Earns A Brand A Pool Of Loyal Advocates Actively Bringing In New Referrals

Customers prefer to do business with brands recommended by their peers—family and friends. In a survey conducted in 2019 by Hubspot—a marketing and software development company, on the state of customer service, 87% of respondents considered reviews and recommendations by friends and family to be more trustworthy than sales or marketing content compared to ten years ago. 10% of the respondents considered marketing content to be trustworthy while only 3% of the respondents considered the sales people to be trust worthy 2. The survey findings are presented graphically hereunder:

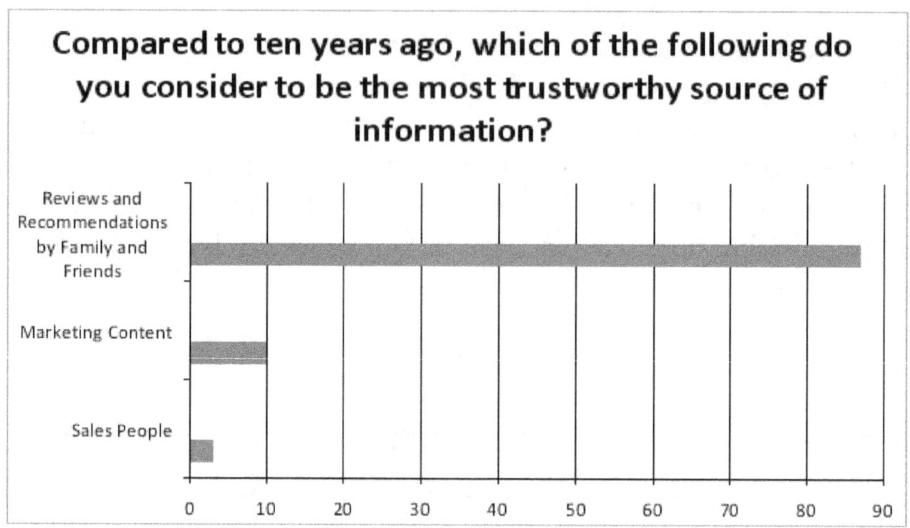

This finding speaks volumes. Peer review and recommendations have become increasingly important in attracting new customers. It therefore follows that creating a flawless experience for your existing customers has become crucial to your future success. Needless to add that delivering an exceptional customer experience is inevitably every company's greatest challenge and strength.

Customer experience goes beyond the single touch point with the brand

Customer experience goes beyond the single touch point with the brand to impact the feelings and customer emotions and encompass the entire customer service journey. *It is not enough to have a customer service department, customer service should be the concern and core mandate of the entire company;* every officer of the organization must embrace the mindset of superior customer service. The entire organization must deliberately serve their customers in a way that positively impacts their journey and interaction with the company. *Every encounter with the company should leave the customer feeling appreciated and valued, with a longing to come again for repeat business.* Walt Disney remarked that:

"Do what you do so well they will want to see it again and bring their friends."

Treat your customers as if your world revolves around them

"Every company's greatest assets are its customers, because without customers, there is no company"

~ MICHAEL LEBOEUF

The secret to sustainable business success is to ensure that your customers are treated as if your world revolves around them. This business approach shall go a long way in building the desired positive image with your customers and the general public and make your brand their go-to choice whenever they are making purchase decisions. Someone remarked quite accurately that:

"Your customer's perception is your reality."

Business Consultant and author Brian Tracy also said that:

"Your company's most valuable asset is how it is known to its customers."

The old saying that *'The customer is king'* is not an empty cliché. The customer is the most important person in any business establishment. He is the real boss who pays the salaries and wages of all the officers of the company. The business is dependent on the customer and the vice versa is not true. The customer can fire everybody from the organization, from the chief executive officer down to the janitor, by simply spending his or her money elsewhere.

It is literally suicidal for a business to treat its customers with disdain and take their patronage for granted. A former managing director of a leading bank in Kenya, was known to be very dismissive of the customers who sought his audience on issues regarding the bank's products and services, it was not long before he himself became a casualty of his own casual approach to leadership and management. By the time the board fired him, he had done considerable damage to the bank's reputation and liquidity. The bank in question was eventually bought off by another bank in a deal approved by the regulator –The Central Bank of Kenya, not so long ago.

Leading brands such as Amazon and Zappos that have heavily invested in their customer experience journeys through consistent provision of service excellence and hi-tech innovations, have permanently redefined the customer service landscape. Their customers in turn have built for them their business brands. *These brands are not at the top by chance—it has taken them considerable time and consistent effort to perfect their philosophy and practice of offering service excellence.*

Such brands have gone beyond engaging in transactional businesses to building ongoing business relationships with their customers. As a result they have won an ever growing army of evangelical customers, increased their sales volumes and revenues, and exponentially grown their shareholder value. Always remember that the company may state its brand promise but ultimately it is the customers who decide whether that brand promise was delivered or not.

Reflection questions:

1) Customers not the company ultimately decide whether a brand promise was kept or not. Discuss.
2) It is not about the multiplicity of the channels and platforms that a company has, the customers only care about their experience on these channels. What is your take on this?
3) Loyal customers are more profitable than customer churn. Discuss.
4) The state of customer service survey conducted in 2019 by Hubspot reveals that 87% of the customers considered reviews and recommendations from their peers and family to be more trustworthy than sales and marketing, compared to ten years ago. How can we take advantage of this finding to drive sales going forward?
5) It is not enough to have a customer service department; customer service should be the concern and core mandate of the entire company. Discuss.

CHAPTER THREE: WHAT IS SUPERIOR CUSTOMER EXPERIENCE?

Whenever a customer interacts with a company either in person or through the multiple technologies based channels or platforms, or website visits or even via traditional marketing channels, the customer invariably forms a perception about that company. This perception can be either positive or negative, but is rarely neutral. The perception and feelings generated as a result of these client interactions with the company staff, company products and services, and the delivery channels is what informs the customer experience.

In simplest terms: ***Customer experience is all about how we make the customers feel when they do business with us.***

Customer experience is basically a function of our customer service offering. Whereas ***Customer service means taking steps to create value to our customers by serving their needs and meeting their expectations,*** customer experience on the other hand is the sum total of the feelings and perceptions the customers get by interacting with our business at each and every touch point.

Customer service is the experience we deliver to our customers, it's the promise we keep to them. It is how we follow through for our customers. And ultimately, the quality of customer service we offer to our customers is what generates their feelings associated with our brand when they do business with us and the perceptions they form about us thereof.

Amazingly, no business ever opens its doors with a promise of delivering apathetic, uninterested customer service, and yet interestingly you don't have to travel far to find a business that delivers just that. Isn't it ironic that good customer service offering is really hard to find given the growing number of companies that claim to provide outstanding customer service?

A study conducted by Lee Resources—a US based research and publishing company, found that ***80% of companies believe they offer superior customer experience but only 8% of their customers believe these companies actually deliver the same***[3] This presents a clear disconnect between the ground reality and companies' own perception. The finding clearly shows that most companies are blind to their own limitations.

◆ ◆ ◆

Customer service is an attitude
not a department

Customer service is a mindset of service readiness that needs to be embraced companywide; confining the same to a customer service department is a misnomer of sorts and is simply self-defeating. Whereas almost every company has a customer service department, rampant customer mishandling, poor quality products and services, unreliable delivery channels among other customer service ills continue to plague the service industry as evidenced by the growing number of customer complaints.

One home truth on customer service is that: **Customer Service is not a department.** Tony Hsieh, the Chief Executive of Zappos ltd —the leading US based online shoe and clothing retailer, said the following:

> *"Customer service should not be a department; it should be the entire company"*

In reality, customer service is an attitude and not a department. The attitude of people displayed by their willingness, readiness and self-drive in taking actions to add value to the customers by serving their needs and meeting their expectations.

Customer service is the job of the entire organization, from the C-suite to the janitor. **A company can only be defined by service excellence when customer service becomes everybody's job.** Companies that continue to confine customer service to a department and designate some employees as customer service officers largely miss out on the spirit and place of customer service in a business.

Customers do expect to have their needs of products and services met by the company regardless of the department or the company unit they contact. They need to have their issues solved without undue referrals and delays. **Customers believe that every employee of the organization has been employed for one purpose only—to serve** *their needs and meet their expectations.* In reality, this is what customer service is all about. Customer service exists for only one purpose: to serve the needs of the customers and meet their expectations, thereby making them feel appreciated and valued as persons.

The need to be treated with dignity and decorum is inbuilt within the genetic makeup of every person; human beings instinctively respond positively to acts of kindness and charity. This need only assumes a greater meaning to people where money is involved in exchange for goods and services.

Every rational person wants the best value for both their time and money. This explains why customers are constantly scouting for options or alternatives and will readily switch their patronage to a competitor who promises to offer better services or sell superior quality products. This presents both an opportunity and a threat to every business. It is an opportunity for businesses that becomes the alternative for the customers, and a threat for the businesses that will not offer the same.

What then is superior customer service?

When we talk of good customer service, we refer to acts of customer service that meets the customer's needs and expectations. Customers come to us because they have needs that they expect us to meet. When we serve the customers and meet those needs in the process, we have given them good customer service.

Superior customer service however means *meeting and exceeding our customer's needs and expectations; it is about offering service excellence to our customers.* Superior customer service is one that keeps the customers coming back, while they spread the word about their experience; it is the magic touch that wins the hearts and loyalty of the customers and endears them to a business. This kind of customer service should be the aim of every business desiring to enjoy sustainable and meteoric growth.

It should be noted that superior customer service cannot come from the demand of bosses; on the contrary, it comes from the basic human desire to take care of others. Actually the spirit of customer service is essentially an inner drive and commitment to go the extra mile to make the customer experience more enjoyable and customer engagement delightful not because someone is asked or ordered or paid to offer the service. Customer Service Consultant and bestselling author Ron Kaufman, describes superior customer service in the following words:

> *Superior customer service is not a procedure to follow but a mindset of purposeful engagement and proactive communication that leads to productive behavior[4]*

It is regrettable to note that businesses have turned a very simple human concept into a catastrophic cliché. Managers *demand* customer service from their frontline employees as if it is merely a performance matrix.

Jon Herstein, the Senior Vice President and Chief Customer Service Officer at Box Inc. opines that superior customer service is all about how a business can take every interaction they have with their customers and use that to improve the organization. He said:

> *"When I think about a great service, it's about how you take every interaction you have with your customer and use that as a way to improve your organization."*

There is continuous need for a business to always invest in customer service improvement. Customers' expectation of our products and service offering is always on the rise. The average customer today is much more informed on the availability of choices and varieties, and has naturally upped his/her expectation of the service standards from the various players.

The ability to deliver in a very competitive market—a level of service that is very consistent, reliable and dependable is no longer good enough. In most industries, the things that were considered great ten years ago are now considered basic. This is why it is important for every business leader concerned with sustainable business growth to ensure that his company stays on the never ending journey of improving customer service standards so that excellence is achieved and maintained.

Truly successful organizations all over the world are taking practical steps to understand their customers better. They strive to create more positive experiences for their customers, to generate greater value for their customers, and to deepen loyalty and build long term relationships with their customers. For such companies ***every customer interaction is treated as an opportunity to build new lasting emotional bond with the customer***. These organizations have internalized this very important business philosophy: ***A satisfied customer is the best business strategy of all.***

These companies always endeavor to keep positive public image by offering quality products and services. That is why management consultant and bestselling author Brian Tracy remarked that:

> *"Your company's most valuable asset is how it is known to its customers."*

As we come to **the end** of this chapter, it is imperative to note that ***people are mostly loyal only to their needs of value and dignity not necessarily to other persons or brands.*** People however become loyal to those brands whose actions and policies demonstrate that they also appreciate the customers' need to be treated with dignity and value. Customers are known to silently vote out industry players who take their patronage for granted, by taking their business to the competition. A business that routinely offers pathetic customer service actively works towards its inevitable closure.

Reflection questions:

1) How would you describe the experience of your customers with your brand?
2) A company can only be defined by service excellence when customer service becomes everybody's job. Discuss.
3) Superior customer service can be either a threat or an opportunity for a business. Discuss.
4) Superior customer service can't come from the demand of bosses. What is your take on this?
5) Offering superior customer experience is a journey, not a destination. Discuss

CHAPTER FOUR: WHAT DO CUSTOMERS REALLY WANT?

"You don't need the resources of Amazon or Netflix to make the moves that will keep your customers coming back for more"

~ILYA POZIN

Great innovations driven by technological advancements have permanently disrupted the consumer market today. Leading companies such as Amazon and Netflix have used state of the art innovations that have redefined the customers' experiences and by extension greatly changed the customers' expectations of service offering by the various industry players.

Whereas it is true that the customers' have upped their expectations of the service experience in terms of speed of service and convenience overtime, it is also true that the customers still want the same things they have always wanted—to be taken care of.

Customers simply want quality products and great customer experience, nothing more nothing less. Granted, they are now more demanding, more informed and much more impatient. They expect their problems to be solved much faster, since technology has availed at our disposal the tools to offer such speeds.

Customers today have become much bolder and louder and are more likely to share their experiences—both positive and negative, with the rest of the world via social media. In a survey conducted in 2019 by Hubspot—a marketing and software development company, on the state of customer service, where they interviewed over 1,000 service professionals in more than five countries, they confirmed that:

> *Customers have a bigger, stronger voice than ever.* **89%** *of customer service professionals agreed that customers are more likely to share positive or negative experiences now than in the past.* **88%** *agreed that customers have higher expectations than in the past, and* **76%** *agreed that customers are smarter and more informed now than they were previously*[5]

It is foolhardy to attempt to compete with the Amazons of this world, since you might not have the resources for the same; however there is something you can still do to win in this war on client acquisition and retention. Why not prioritize on what you can control and still get ahead of the pack?

In this chapter we will explore the most pertinent issues that customers' want as they interact with various business brands. Any business person or entrepreneur who delivers these customers' expectations will definitely steer ahead of the competition and build a formidable brand. You can take cues from the same for actionable initiatives as necessary.

Hereunder are some of the aspects of service that customers crave for:

- *Quality products and efficient services*
- *To be known and understood*
- *Personalized customer experience*
- *Easy access to products and services*
- *Channel-less support*
- *Faster service*
- *Reliable and dependable partners*

a) Quality products and Efficient services

Customers want products and services that meet their specifications; they require products that function the way they need them in order to solve their problems or meet their specific desires. Customers come to us because they have needs—to purchase goods that meet their needs or to procure services that solve their problems.

Customers typically operate on budgets. They want affordability without compromising on quality. Affordability does not necessarily mean cheap; it is about the perceived value derived from the purchase in comparison to the cost involved. The products purchased or services procured should be the efficient solution to the functions and needs the customers are trying to meet. Do therefore ensure that you sell what adds value to your customers.

It is the customers who determine the value they derive from the use of our products and services. Just like when we seek the services of a medical doctor, we expect to be given the correct diagnosis and appropriate prescription of drugs that will cure our ailments. When patients get well after receiving the medical services of a physician, their normal tendency is to go back for repeat services should they experience similar medical challenges in future, and they will most likely recommend the doctor or the clinic to their families and friends.

b)   To be known and understood

Technological advancement has provided more avenues for customers today to connect with a business. Customers today use multiple channels and platforms to contact businesses. Such avenues include calls, e-mail, and chats among others. When they connect with a brand on any one of the channels, they expect to be *known* and be *served on demand* regardless of the channel used.

Repeat customers do expect the company to have their details and spending preferences, gleaned from historical transactions. It is therefore incumbent upon the company to invest in customer data harvesting, storage and use to improve the overall customer experience. This shows the customers that you value their business and take their patronage seriously. So get to know your customers and use that data to make their future interactions worthwhile.

c)   Personalized customer experience

If there is one thing that customers crave for, it is personalized attention—they want to be the centre of attention when they are interacting or transacting with a brand. ***Customers don't really care about your many channels. Instead, they overwhelmingly prefer to have a cohesive and personalized experience they can access wherever they go.*** And increasingly that's what they expect.

Customers interpret personal attention in customer service as being caring. Care makes customers to feel that they have a connection with the company. People naturally prefer to do business with a company that cares for them. Incidentally customers are willing to spend more where they experience personal touch.

*According to a research conducted by Gartner—US based Global Research and Advisory Services firm, on consumer spending habits, **64%** of customers will spend more when there is personalized care versus only **14%** when there is low brand connection.*[6]

It therefore pays to be caring for your customers, to be helpful to them in their shopping experience.

Customer interaction history across all the business touch points helps in delivering relevant, personalized content to your customers, making it easier to connect with your customers. All these add up to an exceptional Customer Experience strategy. Netflix Company for example has succeeded in driving its sales and customer loyalty because its service recommends shows and movies for the customers to watch based on their viewing history. Netflix in essence gives its customers personalized experience and their phenomenal success validates the point that customers do crave personalized experiences.

d) Convenience and easier access to products and services

Customers want convenience and easier access to products and services. This trend has been heavily driven by technological advancement—customers now expect constant availability of the company's products and services on the various channels and platforms for their own convenience. Your delivery channels should therefore avail your products and services nearer to the customers. Your customers need to access your products and services wherever and whenever they so wish, at their convenience.

The idea here is to be available on multiple channels or to have Omni-channels strategy, to be available on whatever channels your customers choose for communicating their needs. Omni-channels strategy enables a brand to sell directly to the customer based on the channel or platform the customers use frequently. While you can closely monitor these communications, let the customers choose the particular channels to use.

e) Channel-less support

> *"All the customer wants is to connect with a company. It's not about a channel. It's about making a connection. So, make it easy. Make it seamless. Make it ubiquitous. Make it channel-less!"*

> – SHEP HYKEN

Beyond your availability on the various platforms or channels that the customers may use to access your products and services, customers in reality only care about their experience in connecting with you. Their concern is not the particular channels themselves. Customers just want to connect and seldom think within the confines of channels. ***The channel is simply a backdrop of their experience, rather than the defining detail.*** This is what has birthed the channel-less support strategy.

The channel-less experience is about building connections around multiple channels with a greater focus of enhancing the customer experience with a given brand. Rather than treating each channel as an island, you think of them as nodes on a network. It is a strategy similar to the Omni-channel or multi-channel support, in that it also endeavors for fluidity; however channel-less approach completely omits the idea of channels altogether, and instead entirely focuses on the customer experience.

Channel-less support seeks to ensure that the experience of the customer with the company at every touch point is consistent regardless of the channel used. It focuses on the brand experience itself, and not where it is taking place. The brand already knows the customer's preferences from the previous interactions and is therefore able to provide a personalized experience regardless of the channel the customer approaches the brand from.

Though channel-less strategy focuses on brand experience, it still requires proper technology and infrastructure that many Omni-channel strategies are built upon.

Your audience is constantly talking; you need to make sure you're listening. This is why support teams need to drop the channels, and keep the focus on resolving customer problems regardless of where they come from. This allows the brand to be more proactive since conversational data is not only collected in one place but is readily available to the service representatives for use in building stronger relationships with the customers. This makes the customers to feel taken care of. Customers feel like they are having one long conversation with a brand—even as they switch from call to chat to e-mail and so forth.

Using the channel-less strategy invariably allows the company to engage their customers more. Highly engaged customers are incredibly valuable as they tend to make more frequent purchases and normally spend more on the particular brand, than when they are less engaged.

Leading companies at the fore front of redefining customer experience are no longer looking at channels in isolation but rather how the channels work together. In other words, they're creating a channel-less experience that's centered on the customer journey.

Even for smaller businesses or startups that can't possibly monitor phone lines and social media messaging every hour of every day, they could still consider having an automated chat function on their websites to help answer the easier questions without the cost of keeping personnel on standby.

Furthermore, customers now consider it critical to have salespersons on standby whenever they need one to talk to.

f)   Faster service

Customers prefer quick turnaround time for all their product and service requests; they want faster service. Nobody likes waiting. Longer queues are no longer fashionable. Customers have become more demanding and increasingly impatient with the service providers. Technology has only served to up the expectation for speed. That's where mobile apps and internet based reliable service portals come in handy.

According to Vala Afshar, the co-author of *The Pursuit of Social Business Excellence*:

***80%** of customers report that receiving an immediate response to a query affects their loyalty to particular brand.[7]*

However speed should not obscure quality. The two should go together as practically as possible, but if one of the two is to be sacrificed, it should not be the quality aspect.

Leading online retailers such as Amazon has shown that it's certainly possible to have quality service that's available quickly, but given the constraints that many startups face, one of these factors must be prioritized over the other. In such cases, quality is the most important factor because skimping on quality will ultimately make it harder to deliver superior customer service down the road. If quality is set aside for the sake of speed, both will inevitably go on a downward spiral.

g)   Reliable and dependable partners

Last but not least is the customers' need for reliable and dependable partners. Not many people have the leisure of time to shop around every time they need to make a purchase or to procure a service. They would prefer to have that one company that they can always count on to get the products or the services they need—at the right price, at the right quality and with no hassles. They need a business partner they can trust. You can purpose to be that go-to business in your industry or sector.

Profitable and long lasting businesses are securely built on the corner stone of trust. When your customers trust your services and the quality of your products, they become loyal to your brand and will purchase particular products and services exclusively from your company.

CUSTOMER SERVICE STATISTICS

Eighty percent of companies believe they offer superior customer experience but only eight percent of their customers believe these companies actually deliver the same.

~LEE RESOURCES

Let's now look at other statistics touching on a variety of issues that affect customers' behavior to really underscore our main assertions of what the customers want:

On customer spending[8]

- **66%** of consumers are willing to spend more with a company they believe provides excellent customer service.
- **41%** of consumers willing to spend more with a company providing excellent service prefer to support smaller companies
- **9%** willing to spend more with larger companies

On the damage done by poor customer service[8]

- **20%** of consumers left a regular service provider due to poor customer service in 2012
- **55%** backed out of a transaction or purchase based on a poor service experience
- **35%** of customers lost their temper with a service representative in the past year (2012)
- **24%** of those who lost their tempers used social media to talk about their experiences with that company

On causes of customer dissatisfaction[8]:

- **78%** of consumers claim they would leave a service provider if a service delivered is different from what is implied
- **77%** of the consumers would leave a service provider if they are handled by unfriendly or impolite customer service agents
- **73%** of the consumers want ease of access to customer service
- **69%** of the consumers want access to faster customer service
- **50%** of the consumers feel it is extremely important that customer service representatives know their client history based on previous interactions

Why companies lose customers[9]

- **9%**- Hived by competition
- **10%** -Other reasons (death, migration etc.)
- **14%** -Unhappy with product quality
- **67%**- Staff indifference

The cardinal reason why companies lose their customers is staff indifference at **67%**; simply put, it is poor customer service. This is followed by inferior products or poor quality products at **14%**, and then other factors such as death and migration follow closely at **10%**. Interestingly the effect of competition on customer attrition when other factors are held constant is the least of the reasons for customer loss at only **9%**.

The good news is that the chief parameter causing customer loss —staff indifference, is within the control of a business. Staff indifference or poor service attitude by the customer facing staff can be addressed by the business to forestall customer loss. We have dedicated **Chapter Six** of this book to discuss how to build a superior service culture within a corporation.

How customers make buy decision[9]

- **19%** -Price
- **36%** -Product Quality
- **45%** -Customer Service

Customers make decisions to buy and use a product or service based on their perception of how that product or service will meet their expectations. This is known as **Perceived Value** (PV). There are three components of PV:

✓ *Product Quality,*
✓ *Customer Service*
✓ *Cost (price)*

The relationship between these components can be expressed in algebraic formula as follows:

$$PV = Product\ Quality + Customer\ Service - Cost$$

When the perceived value is positive, customers readily make a buy decision; the vice versa is also true.

Superior product quality can be achieved through the intentional and consistent application of high quality assurance checks and controls. Superior customer experience can be achieved by inculcating a superior service culture within the company and entrenched through a quality service mindset by all employees. Product price or Cost, being a function of the total production costs plus any other incidental variables, can be managed by addressing the cost of the individual production elements.

Superior customer experience invariably delights and occasionally amazes customers. ***Delighted customers become evangelists of a brand, freely broadcasting how incredible it is to do business with a brand.***

Happier customers are the direct result of offering exceptional customer service that births an amazing customer experience. And since word-of-mouth is very important in attracting new customers, creating a flawless experience for the existing customers has become essential to the brand's future success. Delivering an exceptional customer experience is inevitably every company's greatest challenge and strength.

We reiterate that it's not always easy to provide a seamless, enjoyable customer experience at every touch point. And that the customers now have higher expectations than ever when it comes to customer service. Not only do you need to provide the right answers and working solutions, you also need speed in delivering the same within the surrounding context of each customer's circumstances. However, with the right systems and processes in place, support teams can perform more efficiently and deliver better results.

In **concluding** this chapter, we would like to point out that offering superior customer experience stands out as the major differentiator between the few successful business brands and the mediocre majority. Companies that invest in customer service for the sake of improving their service offering will create a superior experience for their customers and ultimately win in this war on customer acquisition and retention.

Reflection questions:

1) How can your brand give your customers more personalized experiences?
2) Leading companies are moving from Omni-channel strategy to channel-less strategy, how can your brand benefit from this shift?
3) Skimping on service quality for the sake of speed is counter-productive. Discuss.
4) How can your brand leverage on technology and human touch to be the go-to business in your respective industry for the customers' every purchase decision?
5) Delivering an exceptional customer experience is inevitably every company's greatest challenge and strength. Discuss.

CHAPTER FIVE: WHY SUPERIOR CUSTOMER EXPERIENCE IS IMPORTANT

Why bother with service excellence? The answer lies in the outcome—we all want our business ventures to become successful; we all desire to have a larger market share and more revenues from increased sales. We all would want to be the preferred go-to business for the customers whenever they make purchase decisions. We naturally desire to have a sustainable business growth. In addition to these, those who happen to be men and women of goodwill also want to leave a positive legacy of impacting lives and livelihoods for posterity. Interestingly everybody in the increasingly crowded market wants the same things—*the only difference is how each one goes about in achieving the same.*

In the business environment of cutthroat competition, *offering superior customer experience is the only proven business lifeline.* According to one researcher and technology consultant John Bessant, the only differentiator of the few great companies from the mediocre majority is the personal experience that those businesses are able to create in the lives of their customers. He said that:

> *"In a world where things are increasingly becoming commodities (especially services) the real differentiator becomes the personal experience you are able to create in the lives of your customers."*

Customers today demand products, services and experiences that are relevant and that meet their needs and wants in the moment. Furthermore, customers increasingly want to have seamless engagement across multiple trustworthy platforms and channels. *The service provider that excels at personalizing customers' experience without compromising quality would readily win more customers in this war on customer acquisition and retention.* Majority of the customers would readily spend more on such a provider.

A research done by Peppers and Rodgers Group (2009) on customer maturity monitor, found out that:

> *81% of companies with strong capabilities and competencies for delivering superior customer experience are outperforming their competition*[10]

Benefits Of Offering Superior Customer Experience Or Service Excellence

There are indeed many benefits that would accrue to a service provider who becomes more customer-focused and excels in the provision of superior customer experience. The same have already been alluded to in the opening statements of this chapter. The following however are the specific dividends that accrue to a brand as a result of offering service excellence:

i. *Increased sales*
ii. *Increased revenues*
iii. *Enhanced public image*
iv. *Reduced operational costs*
v. *Increased customer satisfaction*
vi. *Customer retention and loyalty*
vii. *Higher conversion rates of online queries*

We shall explore them in depth hereunder:

i. Increased sales

Service excellence results into increased sales. Your current customers are likely to try out other company products and services within your offering range. This results into cross-selling and up selling of your products and services. Your customers become evangelical and will readily refer their friends and families to purchase your products and services –in essence your satisfied customers become your vocal *pro bono* advocates.

ii. Increased revenues

"If you make a sale, you can make a living. If you make an investment of time and good ser-

vice, you can make a fortune"

–JIM ROHM

The cross selling and up selling of your company products and services comes with increased business revenues thus boosting business liquidity. The increased revenue and liquidity can afford the company the wherewithal for growth and expansion.

Superior customer experience ultimately makes more customers to increase their **average order values**. The company also benefits from having a higher **customer lifetime value (CLV)**. Besides, the purchases by the additional stream of referral customers only add to your swelling basket of income.

Furthermore, the positioning of superior customer service allows for higher pricing and hence bigger margins as the customers willingly pay the premium for the exceptional service offering. This results in growth of the shareholder value in step with a company's service reputation in the industry.

For example, the giant Telco, Safaricom ltd is relatively more expensive compared to the other telecommunication service providers in the Kenyan market, and yet most subscribers still prefer to use its services in communication—in voice and data, simply because of its reliability and ready customer support structures.

iii.   Increased Customer satisfaction

Customers come to our business for only one reason—*to have their needs and expectations met.* By focusing on offering service excellence, the needs and expectations of customers are not only met but are regularly exceeded. This makes the customers to feel happy and bask in their self-worth as valuable business partners; your great customer service invariably succeeds in making their day. And as a result thereof, your business becomes their go-to choice for similar future engagements.

iv. Customer retention and loyalty

Superior customer service breeds brand loyalty and customer affinity. The customer will most likely become a source of repeat business and to recommend the business to friends and family members. Your customers become your unpaid brand ambassadors freely broadcasting how incredible it is to do business with you.

When you regularly wow and amaze your customers in your day-to-day dealings with them, your business becomes their go-to choice for every future similar business engagements. It becomes increasingly difficult for any competitor to convince them otherwise.

v. Reduced operational cost

"The more advocates you have the fewer ads you have to buy"

~DHARMESH SHAH

Studies have shown that loyal customers are more profitable than customer churn and that better service is a key factor in retaining your best customers. When your customers are satisfied and have become your business ambassadors, they freely advertise your business for you.

In this era where companies spend millions of dollars in paid advertisement without any guarantee of return on the same investment, having an army of loyal fans turned brand ambassadors freely broadcasting how incredible it is to do business with your brand is a big cost saving strategy. James Cash Penney, an American businessman and founder of J. C Penney Stores noted that:

> *"Courteous treatment of a customer will make the customer a walking advertisement."*

Furthermore, studies have also shown that *it costs at least five times more to acquire a new customer than to retain an existing one*[11]. If you want to save some money and reduce operation costs in your business, then consider investment in offering service excellence.

vi.   Enhanced public image

When a company becomes known for offering superior customer service, the brand image gets a valuable boost. This enhanced public image can become a great buffer providing protection in case there is a slip-up in customer service. *The positive customer reviews helps the business to retain revenue and acquire new customers even in the face of a temporary back clash.*

A prime example of this was witnessed in Kenya when the customers of Chase Bank Ltd stood with the lender at a time when it was facing sanctions from the Central Bank of Kenya, before it was eventually put under receivership by the regulator (for very different reasons). When it was opened for the customers to pick up their deposits, a number of customers actually took more deposits to Chase Bank. Chase bank had succeeded to cut a niche for itself in the SME market in Kenya, and strongly positioned itself as the go-to bank for the SME customers.

Business Consultant and author Brian Tracy said:

"Your company's most valuable asset is how it is known to its customers."

vii.   Improved employees' morale

A culture of service excellence connects the hearts and minds of the employees to the company shared values and practices; when the company emphasizes customer service excellence and all that go into it such as mutual respect for others, understanding and prioritizing the customers' needs, and of going the extra mile; the employees feel and become part and parcel of the company mission and vision. They get the internal motivation to give their best towards the achievement of the company mission and vision.

viii.   Higher conversion rates of online queries

With a greater focus on customer experience, businesses will realize a positive impact on the conversion rates of online queries by the prospective customers. The brand shall also attract increased traffic to its website. This further adds to the enhancement of the company's public image and increased sales.

Superior Customer Experience Should Not Be Limited To The External Customers

Superior customer experience should not be limited to the external customers only, but must of necessity include the internal customers—the employees. Employers and management teams need to give their employees conducive working environment to enhance their micro and macro experiences; this will connect the employees' hearts and minds to the company mission and vision, thus giving them the impetus to give their best efforts in pursuit of the company's common objectives.

Furthermore, employees are now looking for ways to make their work experience more enjoyable; to have cordial working relationships with their colleagues, and to give greater value to their customers. The employers stand to reap immense positive returns by cultivating and maintaining a healthy work environment and supportive human resource policies for its employees. Richard Branson, the founder of Virgin Atlantic, accurately remarked that:

"You take care of your employees and your employees shall take care of your customers"

As we **conclude** this chapter, we would like to point out that major organizations are actually taking practical steps to really embrace the link between offering a high quality customer experience, loyalty and the long-term financial success of the company. As a result more companies are making effort to listen to the feedback of their customers.

In the business environment of cutthroat competition where products and services have become increasingly commoditized, with governments increasing their oversight role thus limiting lee ways that businesses would hitherto legally take advantage of, not to mention the ever increasing risks posed by both globalization and technology, superior customer experience remains the only time tested and guaranteed business strategy for both client acquisition and retention, and the enhanced efficiency that makes leading organizations successful.

Reflection questions:

1) Superior customer experience allows for higher pricing by the

brand. What is your take on this?

2) Offering superior customer experience to your customers inevitably reduces the cost of doing business. Discuss.

3) How can you use customer service as a strategy in client acquisition and retention?

4) Apart from the benefits discussed in this chapter, what other benefits do you think could accrue to a business that excels at offering service excellence?

CHAPTER SIX: SUPERIOR CUSTOMER EXPERIENCE BUILDING BLOCKS

"Building a good customer experience does not happen by accident, it happens by design"

~ CLARE MUSCUTT

Building and maintaining superior customer experience culture does not happen automatically or by chance, on the contrary, it is created by the concerted and deliberate effort of the leadership, management and staff of an organization. The role of the business leaders in building and maintaining this superior service culture cannot be over emphasized. Leadership guru and author Peter F. Drucker observed the crucial role of leadership in everything worthwhile and remarked as follows:

"Only three things happen naturally in organizations: Friction, confusion and underperformance. Everything else requires leadership."

Studies have shown that whereas a majority of companies believe that they offer superior customer experience, only a small fraction of their customers feel that those companies actually deliver the same. As already noted in **Chapter Four**, one such study conducted by Lee Resources—a US based research and publishing company, ***found that 80% of companies believe they offer superior customer experience but only 8% of their customers believe these companies actually deliver the same***[12.] This finding shows that there is a clear disconnect between ground reality and companies' own perception. It also reveals that most companies are actually blind to their own limitations.

However, there is always a silver lining under every dark cloud—*this widespread disastrous customer service offering presents a golden opportunity for forward looking entrepreneurs and business leaders to fill the gap and grow their businesses.* Incidentally, most businesses are delusional in thinking that they are customer service stars, while at the same time their customers are out in the market looking for a better option. You can be that better option, but it won't be easy.

There's a lot that goes into creating and maintaining a superior customer experience culture, you can however start with these seven building blocks:

- *Recruit customer service oriented people*
- *Continuously train and develop your staff*
- *Empower your staff to perform their roles*
- *Hold your people accountable*
- *Recognize and reward the service providers*
- *Leverage on technology*
- *Be proactive*

1. Recruit Customer Service Oriented People

Highly successful companies are very deliberate in their staff selection process. Let's face it, not everyone is cut out for customer service. It takes patience, empathy and above all, an unshakable positive attitude to handle customers with dignity and humility at all times. Your customer facing staff should have the following qualities on the bare minimum:

- *Enthusiasm*
- *Good communication skills*
- *Customer empathy*
- *Patience*
- *Flexibility*
- *Problem solving skills*
- *Company and product knowledge*

You should prioritize these qualities above all else for your team especially your customers' contact team. The rule of thumb is *to Hire for positive customer service attitude and train for skills.*

Business is a journey with a mission and a vision, do therefore hire people who are committed to your service philosophy, who will easily make cultural fit with little training and orientation. These kinds of persons will make your journey enjoyable as opposed to making it tolerable.

2. Continuously Train and Develop your staff

The second parameter is continuous training and development of your team. Take time to train and mentor your staff. Train your people on quality customer service on an on-going basis. It is human nature to forget what we have learnt as time goes by; this implies that the leadership is under obligation to keep the employees always informed on service excellence expectations.

Orient your new staff on superior customer service. Let your new hires experience the best of your customer service culture in action during their first few months on the job. You could also introduce your new hires to your best customers to give them a firsthand experience on how offering superior customer experience builds strong customer and brand relationships. Equally important is the constant need to manage and motivate the new service players on your team.

The grind of daily customer service can cause anyone to lose track of their priorities without help and reminders. Besides, it is not uncommon to encounter customers that are in a foul mood or are just angry or those who simply do not appreciate the efforts of your staff in providing service excellence. This can cause *'wear and tear'* on the service provider. This explains why leading companies with robust customer service cultures continuously train and retrain their team members on offering superior customer service.

The last must-have quality of the customer facing staff in the list in point One —*Good company and product knowledge*—should of necessity be sharpened continually by periodically conducting company and product knowledge trainings. *Orientation training alone is not sufficient to enable the new hires to fully internalize the knowledge of the company and that of its products and services in entirety.*

One way of doing on-the job customer service training is to role-play your most frequent customer objections and to provide a model of your ideal responses. Always remind your team members that their job is to help the customers, as opposed to completing any secondary tasks.

3. Empower your employees to perform their roles

Having selected, trained and deployed your customer service

oriented people, let them know that you expect them to balance the needs of every customer with the needs of the company. Then get out of their way and let them do the work you have hired them to do. Staff productivity and morale goes up when the staff know that they are trusted to make decisions on customer service matters provided they have balanced the customer needs with those of the company. It saves time and money for both the customer and the company.

To truly reach a standard of service excellence you have to give your customer service team the freedom to do whatever it takes to find a final resolution. This could include making a few compromises or spending a little extra to deliver the service excellence promise.

A story is told of a travelling executive who forgot her phone charger in the hotel room in her hurry to catch a morning flight to her next business destination; she planned to contact the hotel about the said charger once she had settled in her destination but was pleasantly surprised to find a small package addressed to her containing her charger and a spare one just in case. The customer service representative in the last hotel noticed the left charger and decided on her own initiative to spend a little more to send the charger together with an extra one (she decided to buy an extra charger just in case) in a parcel to the destination address of their esteemed customer. This hotel just won themselves a new loyal evangelical customer with this rare gesture of outstanding customer service.

Empowering your employees with the authority and the requisite resources to deliver on the promise of excellent service is a guaranteed way of ensuring that customers are satisfied with the company service offering. It beats logic to hire, train and deploy smart customer service oriented staff only to micro-manage them in their day-to-day duties.

4. Hold your people accountable

As a leader, you still take the full responsibility of ensuring there is consistent superior service offering in your company. This implies that you have to hold all your employees accountable if over time they can't or won't deliver the kind of service that your customers deserve.

Apparently even if you are an all-star recruiter and trainer, some recruitees for whatever reasons are just not going to consistently deliver the kind of service that will set your company apart, making it the hub of superior customer service offering that you aspire. These employees won't see the importance of service excellence in the same way that the rest of the team does. Reach out to these employees and make sure that they have the tools they need to succeed. When your best attempts to help them to improve their customer service still do not yield the expected results, you can release them to find their passion elsewhere.

5. Recognize and reward the service providers

In a strong service environment *recognition and reward* must come more frequently from the company as the customers seldom appreciate and reward great service. What gets recognized and rewarded gets repeated. Celebrate milestones in improved customer service offering. You can recognize and reward your most improved department, most helpful colleague, or any outstanding customer service actions from your team members. The rewards and recognition can include public acknowledgment of the staff or the department involved, issuing a letter of commendation with or without monetary component, among other measures.

More importantly, build superior customer service culture in your reward and disciplinary decisions. For example, outstanding customer service rating should inform a bigger portion on the staff promotion criteria. Equally your team should be made aware in no uncertain terms that the leadership doesn't tolerate inferior or pathetic customer service in all its forms.

6. Leverage on technology

Use technology to provide convenience to your customers. Ensure your business is accessible by the customers on the various platforms and channels afforded by the technology. As already noted elsewhere in this book, technological advancement has provided more avenues for customers today to connect with a business. Customers today use multiple modes of communication including e-mail, chats, call and other social media avenues to contact businesses. Ensure there are assigned personnel to attend to the customer queries in a timely manner regardless of the channel used. Wherever applicable, inbuilt auto responders could be used on the company websites to respond to common queries.

Technology has equally provided new product and service delivery channels. Ensure the availability, reliability and the safety of those technology-enabled delivery channels by investing in robust IT systems and processes. Such delivery channels include online sales and payments portals, POS devices, credit cards etc.

Technology is indeed a timely tool that can be used to drive down costs and upscale sales. However *use technology only as a business enabler; under no circumstances should you let technology to obscure your human interaction with your customers.*

7. Be proactive

"Get closer to your customers, so close that you tell them what they need before they know it

themselves."

~ STEVE JOBS

Customers do appreciate when you are forward looking and proactive in providing solutions to their needs. It is no longer fashionable to just react to the problems if you are to be a cut above the rest. This is only possible when you get close enough to your customers and understand them.

Taking own initiative to contact your customers either when a problem arises before they have a chance to contact you on the same, or to inform them on the emerging issues that are likely to affect them in one way or another, shows your customers that you are prioritizing their best interests and acting with urgency because they are important to you.

If you are in the financial services sector for example, your clients look up to you for advice on a variety of issues; do your best therefore to stay informed on what is happening in the industry and the economy in general to be in a position to give sound advice to your customers on the timely actions they could take to safeguard their businesses or to mitigate risks as the case may be.

This type of vigilance is what separates a great service organization from the mediocre majority.

As we come to the **end** of this chapter, we would like to point out that there is still a huge opportunity for business growth and the creation of lasting positive legacies in the business world today. You can take the right steps to make sure that your team consistently delivers an awe-inspiring service; and the result will a shot at greatness. Your customers are waiting.

Reflection questions:

1) What qualities do you consider most critical when making hiring decisions?
2) In what practical ways can you empower your customer service team to do whatever it takes to solve customer service related issues?
3) What practical ways can you use to hold your employees accountable in offering superior customer service?
4) Recognizing and rewarding service providers helps improve customer service offering, how can you use this measure to build superior service culture in your organization?
5) What practical steps can you take to ensure that your team gives awe-inspiring service to your customers?

CHAPTER SEVEN: CARDINAL SINS IMPEDING SERVICE EXCELLENCE

"It takes months to find a customer, but it only takes seconds to lose one"

–VINCE LOMBARDI

It is common knowledge that customers rarely get outstanding customer experience or even the desired customer service. The industry is littered with many customer complaints and disappointments from the various service providers. The advent of social media has only served to give the more vocal customers new and wider avenues for venting out their frustrations. The majority of the customers however still choose to walk away in silence only to take their business elsewhere. This ought not to be the case.

Hereunder this book highlights a few cardinal sins or barriers to watch out for and correct in the never ending journey of pursuing service excellence:

- *Internal politics*
- *Staff indifference*
- *Lack of attention to the customer needs*
- *Lack of commitment to follow up on customer issues*
- *Inexperienced and incompetent staff*
- *Poor delivery channels*
- *Lack of team work*
- *Non-storage of customer data and insufficient use of existing customer data*

1. Internal politics

"In weak companies politics win; in strong companies, best ideas do."

~STEVE JOBS

This book considers internal politics as the first cardinal sin because of its malignant and cancerous nature; this sin is capable of sabotaging even the strongest of goodwill of the most enthusiastic customer service representatives in an organization.

Organizational politics is the intentional and disproportionate enhancement of self-interests at the expense of the larger organization goals. It is a game of self-preservation played by the self-appointed company gate keepers at the expense of the common good. It is self-serving and almost always hits a *Waterloo* moment sooner or later.

The work culture rife with internal politics is characterized by incessant blame games and finger pointing, mind games and malevolent manipulation, avoidance of responsibility and the occasional setting up of people to fail. Honesty in such settings is considered a threat by the self-appointed gate keepers; and the managers operate by pressure or intimidation as opposed to inspiration and offering support to their subordinates.

Furthermore, there is excessive control and micromanagement of the staff. Vital information that should aid customer service provision is withheld from the service providers. Not to mention the open favoritism and nepotism leading to resentment and resignation of those receiving the short end of the stick.

Where internal politics is allowed to take the center stage at the expense of service excellence resulting into rampant customer frustrations, the end game is always massive loss of business opportunities and stagnated growth. The other adverse effects include but are not limited to the following:

- ✓ The active muzzling of staff creativity and spontaneity.
- ✓ Silencing of the great ideas that could otherwise propel the company to the next level, to ensure they never see light of day, since they are considered a threat to the interests of the powers that be.
- ✓ Loss of the best talent to the competition
- ✓ Increased staff attrition
- ✓ Increased operational costs incurred in the subsequent recruitment and training of replacement staff.
- ✓ Customers' dissatisfaction and disappointment by having to explain themselves all over again to the new employees assigned to them. Most of the times, the customers register their disapproval of the ensuing poor service by simply taking their business elsewhere.

It is simply unfathomable to note that whereas most companies promise excellent customer service to their external customers, they in turn allow internal politics to frustrate the employees' good intentions to deliver the same.

To address this malady, the leadership could consider a number of actions:

i.   First the leadership needs to **be very intentional and**

deliberate in fostering a work culture of excellence (You can get your copy of the book *Business Success Beyond Profit: Building a corporate culture of excellence*, by the same author for more information on how to build corporate culture of excellence). Inculcating a corporate culture of excellence within the entire fabric of the company will eliminate this vice, and in its place put a customer-centric working culture with a very productive team spirit to boot.

ii. **Lead from the front.** Your actions and attitudes are the best example of the culture you espouse for your company. Your actions and behavior will work to either reinforce the company core values or to actively veto the same. Your subordinates are keenly observing you and taking cues from your everyday work behavior and using the same as the expected and acceptable standard of conduct or norm for the company. Therefore be very intentional about your leadership style.

iii. **Be firm and fair in your decisions and everyday dealings with your employees.** In leadership, leaders get the work behavior they are willing to tolerate. When it comes to your attention as a leader that there are narcissistic members within your ranks, take timely decisive actions on such staff including dismissal when a positive change is not forthcoming. Keeping such toxic members in your company will do more harm than good to your work environment.

Doing Memos, or simply talking about stopping this vice will remain just that—*mere talk*. Your firm actions will serve to communicate in no uncertain terms your resolve to stamp out the vice.

iv. **Take mentorship and career growth seriously**. Everyone needs to feel that they are learning and growing in their work. The company needs to invest in the growth and development of her employees as this helps to uplift the staff spirits and create team coherence; the employees will then become fully engaged in the tasks at hand. On the contrary, when people feel that they are falling behind in their careers, they become suspicious and nervous, and this is a ripe mindset for engaging in office politics.

v. **Encourage workplace friendships**: encourage voluntary, smaller and affordable workplace outings and team bonding events such as group lunches or dinners, interdepartmental or unit sports etc. People become less inclined to play underhand political games when colleagues whose opinions they care about will get to know of the same or shall be negatively affected in one way or another.

vi. **Avoid "managerial mystique"**: Managerial mystique is the tendency of the managers to make decisions that impact the work or careers of the employees without explaining themselves to the affected staff. This practice is a recipe for breeding mistrust and suspicions among staff often leading to formation of factions within the company. Do endeavor to explain sensitive or difficult decisions, especially if they affect how people work.

vii. Last but not least, **clearly draw the lines between work and personal/family issues**. It is not a crime to employ acquaintances or people close to you in one way or another; however these persons should neither be allowed nor encouraged to use their privileged backgrounds to take undue advantage over the rest, as this invariably results in factions at work place and resentments among those receiving the short end of the stick.

Always remember the weighty words of legendary inventor and businessman Steve Jobs: *"in weak companies politics win; in strong companies, best ideas do."* Then decide how you want your company to be perceived.

2. Staff indifference

"The reputation of a thousand years may be undermined by the conduct of one hour" ~ Japanese proverb

The attitude of the customer service agent towards the customer is extremely important. Simply put, the quality of the personal interaction between the service representative and the customer always has the biggest contribution on how the customers evaluate their experience with the given brand. This personal touch or lack of it thereof plays a bigger role than any other technical aspects that may form part of the service offering. ***The damage caused in the customer experience as a result of staff indifference can hardly be salvaged by either good quality products or great delivery system however impeccable that might be.***

Whenever the customer-facing-staff displays an attitude of indifference to the customers, it becomes an automatic put off to the customer; it invariably breeds contempt and creates a negative impression on the customers.

To address this malady, the leadership and management should always be on the lookout for such unbecoming attitude in its ranks, among their staff members to forestall any likely damage thereof. This can be done by establishing clear feedback channels for the customers and taking timely corrective actions as the case may be. Mystery shopping by the leadership can also be employed to get a firsthand experience of your company customer service in action.

3. Lack of attention to the customer needs

One of the leading qualities every customer service agent should have is the ability to listen to the customers. Active listening to understand the customers' issues enables the service agents to give the customers appropriate solutions.

It is unwise to presume that you know what the customer wants; instead you should hear them out. Customers simply expect to be heard and understood. ***Even if the customers are wrong, let them be wrong with dignity.*** They also expect the service agents to listen to their complaints, compliments, feedback and any suggestions they might have; they equally expect you to take these feedback and suggestions seriously and act on ***them.*** It is almost considered criminal to be engaged on other things when a customer is talking to you as a service representative.

How would you feel if you arrived at a new restaurant and the waiter scarcely listened to your order and in no time brought to you food that you never ordered? Or if you walked into a bank to open an account for your registered business that needs to make payment to suppliers using cheque leaves, with the occasional need to be accommodated by the bank with overdraft facilities when your liquidity is temporarily miss-aligned, only for the ac-count opening officer at the bank to open for you an ordinary savings account (with no such product features)? Well, that's the kind of damage the service providers often subject the customers to whenever they fail to listen to them to adequately understand their service requests.

To address this malady, the business leadership should train the staff especially the customer contact team on effective communication skills with emphasis to give the customers their full attention whenever they are interacting with the customers. Holding routine refresher training courses on customer service is crucial for the maintenance of service excellence, since the grind of daily customer service can cause anyone to lose track of their priorities without help and reminders.

4. Lack of commitment to follow up on customer issues

Many times customers' issues require follow up, either with the head office or other departments. This is especially true when the service or product offering requires the input of other employees or different departments. In such circumstances, the customers normally ask the service representative the duration of time their issues will likely take before being resolved, and most times they leave with a *'commitment'* of a specified timeline.

Whereas it is expected that the service representative or their supervisors will see into it that the issue is followed up to its amicable conclusion, this is unfortunately not always the case. Normally the customer will come or call back to check on the progress of their issues only to be tossed around or given indefinite answers as the waiting period continues. What is lacking here is the necessary commitment to follow through the customer issues to their logical conclusion, and that is very frustrating.

To address this malady, the business leadership and management should ensure that their staff members appreciate their primary role in the company, which is to help the customers. *The employees should understand that their primary role is to help the customers as opposed to finishing any secondary tasks.*

Leading companies have put in place compliance monitoring systems that self-escalate customer issues to the next level if they are not resolved within some pre-determined timelines. But more importantly, the service representatives in these leading companies are adequately trained on the importance of rigorous follow up of customer issues; they are equally made to appreciate how this follow up or lack of it thereof impacts the overall customer experience with the brand.

Having a dedicated resource person to ensure effective follow up is done could also be considered wherever appropriate.

5. Inexperienced and incompetent staff

Having adequate product knowledge is very necessary in offering service excellence. Definite knowledge of the internal processes and procedures pertinent to product and service offering shall go a long way in reducing or eliminating customer mis-information by service agents.

When customers have been properly advised on the appropriate products and services relevant to their circumstances and have been given the correct timelines, they mostly make informed choices and have realistic expectations from the company as a result thereof.

Every business should put mechanisms in place to ensure that key touch points of service delivery have competent and knowledgeable staff; *it is simply inexcusable for the customers to get poor service or 'raw deal' so to speak, because the employees handling their issues are either inexperienced or incompetent.*

Having adequate product knowledge alongside the applicable internal policies and procedures, prepares an employee to give the required service to the customers. Whereas it is not a crime to be inexperienced as an employee, it is simply inexcusable not to take personal initiative to learn and master the range of the company products and services plus the applicable policies and procedures in a timely manner. Failure of an employee to understand and appreciate the aforementioned essentially perpetuates incompetence and is therefore an inexcusable sin.

It is recommended that the company should conduct proper and adequate induction for their new employees, as well as ongoing refresher trainings on the products and services, together with other trainings on any emerging issues affecting the employee's work and industry. This shall go a long way in fostering the provision of service excellence to the customers and improvement of the overall customer experience with a given brand.

6. **Poor delivery channels**

> *"In a world of internet customer service, it's important to remember that your competitor is only one mouse click away."* ~ Doug Warner

Technology has ushered in an era of a wide variety of product delivery platforms and channels. Your customers want your presence on all the applicable channels. Customer experience can be dealt a major blow when such technology-enabled channels are neither reliable, nor user-friendly nor safe. *Yes the technical aspects do matter in the overall customer experience since the customers do want to have seamless engagement across multiple trust-*

worthy platforms and channels. Customers highly appreciate the convenience afforded to them by these platforms; do therefore ensure that their convenience is least disrupted.

Have a stand-by technical team to rectify any hitches if and when they do arise.

Taking care of the technical side of customer care is not so difficult, but it requires time and dedication. As already noted elsewhere in this book, the service provider that excels at personalizing their customers' experience without compromising on quality, would readily win more customers in this war on customer acquisition and retention.

Maybe it is time to put yourself in your customer's shoes and try accessing those channels occasionally. This will help you to get first experience with your service offering and help you get answers too such questions as: How easy to navigate are they? How fast is the response from your core system or your service representatives?

Whatever it takes, simply invest in robust delivery channels to enhance the overall customer experience with your brand.

7. Lack of team work

> *"The truth is that teamwork is at the heart of great achievement"* ~ *John C Maxwell*

Customers do not necessarily care about the varied titles of the employees or the different departments they may be working in, all they need is to have their issues sorted. As a matter of fact, customers actually believe that all the company employees are in employment for only one reason—*to serve the needs and expectations of the customers.* They therefore expect seamless service regardless of the necessary escalations that may be applicable, or the many different faces they may meet during their interaction with the company.

Disappointment and customer frustration normally arises when different staff members give conflicting advice to the same customer on the same issue, or when different service representatives give different interpretations of the company policy to the same customer(s).

This malady of lack of teamwork can be cured by having continuous staff training on company policies, products and services to ensure that all staff read from the same page, and by fostering a healthy spirit of team work. Other measures that could be considered include: Instituting a corporate reward mechanism like recognizing and rewarding the most improved department or branch; having team building outings to aid staff bonding with one another. Additionally a company could consider incorporating departmental or unit performance scores to form a portion of the individual team members overall performance during appraisals; some leading companies actually apportion up to **40%** of the individual's score to team performance and only **60%** to individual's own performance.

It is imperative for you as a leader to ensure that your team is not only strong but that they also give consistent experience to your customers. All team members should work in cooperation, while appreciating that *'a chain is as strong as its weakest link.'* Always endeavor to unite your team by inspiring them to see the bigger picture and to give their best to the customers.

8. **Non-storage of customer data and insufficient use of**

the same

We have already noted that customers today use multiple platforms and channels to contact the business; and when they do connect, they expect to be known and to be served on demand regardless of the channel or platform used. They expect their communication from the various sources to be treated by the company as one continuous conversation. It is extremely important to the customer that the company not only have access to their previous transactions history and their personal details, but that the company also makes appropriate use of the same in enriching their personal experience with the brand.

It is sad to note that some companies either by acts of commission or omission, do not properly harvest or use the previous customer transactional data and personal details. This comes at a huge inconvenience to the customers and of course loss of valuable business opportunities for the company involved. *Kindly note that the degree to which customers' information is used by the company to provide a personalized solution is in direct correlation with the degree to which customers perceive their support interaction as quick and easy.* Failure to collect the customer information or collecting but not making proper use of the same are both detrimental to how customers perceive a brand support.

Companies that have perfected the art of collating customer information and making proper use of the same to customize service solutions to their customers have a distinct advantage over those that don't. For example, an hotel that meticulously saves and shares even the minute details of the customers' preferences such as type of beverage they drink or the specific dishes they have ordered in the past, will endear itself to its customers as valuable life-long partner in the hospitality industry.

Imagine how it feels if you are the customer and you had to re-introduce yourself and bring copies of your identification documents to your credit officer or your lawyer every time you required their services!

Make sure that you are asking your customers only for the information which is needed and you are using it to the maximum to provide better services to them. This implies that the company should of necessity invest in appropriate customer data harvesting and use of the same in enriching the customers' experience with the brand.

As we **conclude** this chapter, we would like to point out that the above list of service barriers is by no means exhaustive; these 'sins' made it to the list to assist the service providers to do an introspection on areas that they may need to work on. The pursuit of service excellence is a never ending journey; it requires continuous improvement as we aim for perfection. Even if you have already eliminated these 'service ills', it's no time to rest on your laurels. There is still a lot of work to do to stay ahead of the pack.

Reflection questions:

1) Looking at the cardinal sins impeding service excellence, which areas presents your company's weakest points?
2) How does your brand measure the customer satisfaction levels?
3) Leading companies have put in place compliance monitoring systems that self-escalate customer issues to the next level if they are not resolved within some pre-determined timelines. What is the practice in your company?
4) How would you describe the effectiveness of your induction trainings and the subsequent refresher trainings? How could they be improved upon?
5) Team work is key consideration in delivering consistent customer experience in the entire company; in what ways can you foster effective team work among your staff?

CHAPTER EIGHT:
THE FIVE LEVELS OF CUSTOMER SERVICE

The Changing Expectations Of Consumers

We live in a world where customer expectations are constantly evolving. For this reason, customer service is by no means static but is rather fluid with the never ending need to always invest in its improvement. Customers are increasingly demanding curated experiences, seamless interaction and immediate satisfaction.

It therefore follows that *the ability to deliver in a very competitive market, a level of service that is very consistent, reliable and dependable is no longer good enough.* With more information than ever at the customers' fingertips, they now have more control of how, when and where to interact with the business brands.

For any business to succeed and thrive in the market, the business must have the ability to satisfy its customers by meeting their needs and or exceeding their expectations. The good news however is that the fundamentals of customer service the world over regardless of the industry involved are still the same—*It is all about taking steps to take care of other people.*

◆ ◆ ◆

The Levels Of Customer Service Offering

The changing customer needs and the degree of their satisfaction by various service providers has brought to the fore the need to categorize customer service into various levels. Granted every organization offers some levels of customer service, but we all agree that these service levels differ from one company to another. Whereas an increasing number of companies claim to give outstanding customer experience to their clientele, most of their customers' feedback and sentiments are not in support of such claims.

Interestingly most of these companies' products and services are more or less commoditized, with similar delivery systems or channels. Therefore the main differentiator for the businesses in whichever industry is undoubtedly their customer service standards.

Leading customer service consultants have attempted to categorize customer service into various levels, premised on the ability of the service providers to meet the expectations of their customers. Majority of these consultants generally concur on the use of a **five point scale differentiator** –with **One (1)** being the being the lowest or simply bad customer service and **Five (5)** being the highest or excellent customer service. These levels have been assigned various descriptive names that vary with different service consultants. This book takes a similar approach and has assigned each level a descriptive name commensurate with the customer satisfaction at that level:

- *Level One: Pathetic Customer Service*
- *Level Two: Basic Customer Service*
- *Level Three: Desired Customer Service*
- *Level Four: Outstanding Customer Service*
- *Level Five: Unbelievable Customer Service*

Level One: Pathetic Customer Service

This is simply bad customer service. It is poor, terrible, irritating, nauseating customer service. It is simply unacceptable for any reason. *At this level the service provider displays apathy, open indifference or outright disdain towards the customers.* The service provider openly blames the customers for any misunderstandings. In some instances the service provider could shout at the customer, bang the table in fits of rage or do other similar ugly things. Some actions of the service provider at this level could even be considered criminal.

At this level, customer expectations are not met, and customers' complaints are rampant. The likely consequence of this kind of service is the loss of customers and eventual business closure.

Examples of such service include: rude employees who show open contempt towards customers—an action that is very rampant in the public transport sector; and willful misrepresentation of facts by company sales representatives to induce customers to buy products they neither need nor have use for.

<u>Hereunder is a personal incident exemplifying this kind of customer service:</u>

In the year 2012, as a branch head of credit of a financial institution, I took my credit team for a get together dinner in a certain restaurant to appreciate them for a week of great productivity, having surpassed the weekly performance targets. I had informed the restaurant manager on phone about our planned dinner at their facility and even gave him a rough estimate of the number of guests to expect, some two hours earlier.

However this dinner being rather an impromptu one, a few staff members who had made prior arrangement for alternative engagements elsewhere could not avail themselves. As it were, those who were able to attend came and we had a good time. When it was time to settle the bill, the restaurant manager insisted that we had to pay for the *meals of those who had not showed up*, arguing that they had used our number (given on phone) to prepare the meals; never mind that I was paying from my pocket. In high fits of rage, he proceeded to bang the table on me. I obliged and paid as he demanded. That was my last time in that restaurant. *I was not surprised to learn that the restaurant closed down within a year of that unfortunate incident.*

Level Two: Basic Customer Service

This is the normal or the usual customer service standard following the established industry code of conduct. Here the service providers do only what is normally expected of them; they simply follow the standard industry practice. Someone would even say that the service providers serve by the book at this service level.

This is the minimum service level required to stay in business—it is the level required for business survival. At this level the service offering is commoditized and standards are at a minimum. Customer expectations are met at this level and the customers have no complaints.

Even though the customers are satisfied for the moment at this level, their loyalty does not exist. Customers can quickly become ex-customers should a worthy competitor come by, who can demonstrate that it can do more than merely meet the expectations of the customers. Moreover, should the service provider fail to meet their expectations at any one point, customers will leave and give their loyalty to someone else who can.

At this level the customers do not feel any emotional connection with the business. Their continued patronage is a function of their convenience. Customers do not feel obliged to share their experiences as they find nothing uncommon or phenomenal in your service offering to talk about.

Examples of basic customer service include:

- Having working and reliable hot shower systems in hotels
- Financial service providers sending bank account statements via e-mail to their customers on routine basis
- Banks having ATM services to enable customers to access banking services beyond the normal working hours

Level Three: Desired Customer Service

At this level, the service provider goes the extra mile by doing something that is totally unexpected but is pleasantly surprising. The service provider goes beyond the norm by doing more, by displaying an attitude of concern. They exceed their customers' expectations by giving their customers pleasant surprises. The customers consider the services as 'satisfactory' or 'generally good'.

At this level of desired customer service, a business begins to experience some degree of success as opposed to mere survival. A business is also able to anticipate its customers' needs and prepare to meet them beforehand at this level. Besides, the service providers are always available at their customers' service.

Exceeding your customers' expectations will gain you some level of customer loyalty and give you an edge over your competitors. ***The good news is that customers are often willing to pay a premium for the kind of service that exceeds their expectations***. This gives the service provider the leeway to increase prices and thereby improve their profit margins.

The leading telecommunication service provider in East Africa —Safaricom ltd, has perfected the art of giving pleasant surprises to its customers. One morning on my birthday, I woke up and found an SMS from Safaricom ltd; the giant Telco had offered me 1 GB of free data to celebrate my birthday. It was such a pleasant surprise that endeared me more to the company.

Offering faster turnaround time beyond what you promised the customer and or doing phone call follow up to ensure customer satisfaction can put you in this category.

Level Four: Outstanding Customer Service

This is where you delight your customers. It is the kind of customer service that not only exceeds customers' expectations but also actually puts a smile on their faces. It is beyond 'satisfactory' and is a big jump from good.

This level of service makes your customers to feel special. Most industry players call this *'giving your customers a wow experience'*. It is rare kind of service. ***Offering outstanding customer service makes your customers to think highly of your company, and to consider it as a great company***.

This level of customer service creates emotional bond with customers. The customers' needs and expectations are not only met and exceeded but they are also touched emotionally by the service provider. This results in true customer loyalty. It becomes extremely difficult for any other industry player to poach them.

When delighting your customers becomes your service standard, you inevitably create an exceptional and highly profitable business. Nothing shows that you care for your customers more than giving them delightful experiences that put smiles on their faces. The legendary customer service consultant and author Brian Tracy, said that:

> *"The greater your success in delighting your customers and providing good customer service, the greater success you will enjoy in your business."* [13]

An example of outstanding customer service was shared by Peter Shankman, an author and business consultant who jokingly sent a tweet to Morton's Porterhouse to meet him at the Newark airport, his destination in two hours' time, since he knew he was scheduled to arrive past the hours that would normally allow him to get restaurant services. To his surprise, a gentleman from porterhouse met him at the airport with a bag containing the porterhouse steak, shrimp, napkins and silverware. Knowing that Peter was a regular customer and having tracked down his arrival details, Morton's traveled more than 23 miles to deliver his food and with – one of the greatest customer service stories of all time.

Here is the famous tweet[14]:

The case of the hotel customer representative discussed in **Chapter Six**, who had noticed that a customer had left her phone charger in her hotel room while in a hurry to catch a morning flight to her next business destination, and packaged it in a parcel with an extra one just in case, and promptly sent the parcel to the customer's next destination even before the customer could call them on the same, is another example of outstanding customer service.

Level Five: Unbelievable Customer Service

This is the apex of customer service excellence. Here you not only exceed your customers' expectations and delight them, but you also amaze them. This level of service results in heartfelt and reminiscing memories for the customer. It is an awesome and breathtaking kind of service. ***The emotional connection created by this level of service is life-long and can't be broken.*** You become the industry benchmark for superior customer service. Other industry players are compared to you. Some service consultants refer to this level as 'Trade mark'.

At this level of customer service you build a legion of evangelical customers who enthusiastically and actively seek new converts to join 'their company'. ***The emotional connection created at this level is so strong that the customers believe and act as part and parcel of your organization.***

Ron Kaufman, a customer service consultant and author of best-selling book *Uplifting Service*, shared an experience of unbelievable customer service in one of his podcasts. Ron lives in Singapore, on the 26th floor of a high-rise apartment. He travels a lot and often uses *taxi* services to get to the airport and other places that do not require a flight. On this day he had a flight to catch by Six o'clock in the morning and had informed his regular taxi service provider firm to collect him by Five O'clock in the morning, in time for the scheduled flight.

Since he had had a long day, Ron requested the customer representative to wake him up by 4.30a.m to enable him to prepare. Unfortunately he put the handle of the house telephone wrongly after talking with the service representative and promptly fell into a sound sleep at 11.30 p.m. When the service representative attempted to contact Ron as agreed, the phone was not going through.

Ron says he was woken up from a deep slumber by a knock at his door, only to check the time and find it was 4.50 a.m. The unusual visitor explained that he had come to wake Ron up so as to get ready for the flight, stating that his phone calls were not going through.

When the customer service representative realized that Ron's phone was not connecting, she reasoned that there must be a technicality somewhere. She went out of her way to locate a taxi driver nearby who could be willing to go up the 26 floors and wake up Ron in time, to prepare and catch his flight. The mistake was fully Ron's but the service representative did what she did not have to do all the same—and with that was one of the most unbelievable customer service stories of all time.

By regularly amazing your customers, you propel your business to the position of market dominance. You leave behind the competition and play in your own league. You thus achieve remarkable revenue growth and sustained profitability.

NB: The quest for customer service excellence is a never ending journey. No matter how you and your company rates on the five levels of service, you can't afford to sit on your laurels. There is always the need for continuous improvement through training and coaching. Even if your customers already consider you the service champions and rate your service as either outstanding or unbelievable, to remain on top of the game, you will need to continuously remind your team through regular refresher courses on customer service excellence.

Reflection questions:

For this chapter, some of the questions have two parts—one is on a company level and the other on an individual level. These questions are also valid for those who only serve internal customers—fellow staff or other departments of the same organization.

1. Where would you rate your company and yourself as an individual on this five point scale of customer service?

2. Where would your customers rate your company and yourself as an individual on this five point scale of customer service?

3. Would you give examples of companies in your industry whose customer service could be assigned to each of these levels of service?

4. Which companies outside of your industry could you assign to each of these levels of
service?

5. What do the companies who have 'Outstanding' and 'Unbelievable' service levels (both inside and outside of your industry) do that you could emulate?

6. If you are not already at the 'Unbelievable' level – and very few companies are – what
would you do differently to get close to this level?

CHAPTER NINE: HANDLING CHALLENGING CUSTOMERS

There will always be some customers who for one reason or another will be disappointed by the quality of your products and services, the delivery channels or the quality of the customer service they have received from your company. In some instances, some customers may simply be having bad days or in a foul mood and may choose you as the object of venting their anger and frustrations. Some may choose to express their disappointment and frustrations either through angry outbursts, or by becoming overly emotional or even by using abusive language.

In some instances, due to the perceived intensity of their loss or helplessness in the face of disappointment, some customers may simply become unresponsive or appear truly confused.

The tenets of superior customer service dictates that you should remain professional and calm at all times regardless of the level of provocation you may receive from these encounters. Even if the customer is plainly out of step, staying calm and composed will enable you to mitigate any further damages the service slip-up or the disagreement might cause.

When handling such customers, *always remember to refer to them by their names.* Calling customers by their names has a powerful psychological calming effect on them no matter how angry or agitated they may be.

Hereunder we will give some tips of handling these challenging customers.

Tips Of Handling Challenging Customers:

- *Stay calm*
- *Don't take it personally*
- *Practice active listening*
- *Actively empathize*
- *Apologize gracefully*
- *Find a solution*

We shall briefly elaborate on the above tips hereunder:

i. Stay calm

Don't argue with the customers, simply stay calm. *Remember you*

can win the argument but definitely lose the customer. It is not possible to win both the argument and the customer. Unfortunately, the lost customer will not go away alone, he/she will go away with other customers within his or her circle of influence.

Trying to prove that you or the company is right and the customer is wrong will actually do more harm than good. ***Just assume in a moment of time that all your customers are keenly watching your response.*** Never respond in kind, nor answer fire with fire.

ii.   Do not take it personally

Most of the time chances are that your customer is angry about a bad product or service, and you're just the unfortunate target of their frustration. The customer might call you some unprintable names, or use all the negative adjectives to describe your customer service standards or the company as a whole; but don't take it personally. Just understand that they are describing the bad service or poor quality product and not you as a person.

iii.   Practice active listening

Give the customer your full attention. Hear them out and seek to understand their issue well. Do not attempt to disrupt them. Let them vent it out. The longer they speak it out, the more their anger dissipates. To show the customers that you are truly listening, do repeat what the customer has said.

You could say things such as:

So Mr. Patrick, you are saying that your loan facility has delayed, and that as result, you are likely to miss the deadline for the payment of this semester's examination fees, right Mr. Patrick?

Or

Madam Jane, you are saying that the building materials you ordered and paid for last week have not been delivered on site? And your foreman is concerned that the work might have to stop if no new supplies are delivered on site by tomorrow morning? Is that correct Madam Jane?

iv.   Actively empathize

Put yourself in the customer's shoes. Understand they point of view. You could say things like:

Mr. Patrick, I understand your frustration, if I were you, I would also react the same way.

or

Madam Jane, this must be so hard for you, I truly understand

v.   Apologize gracefully

Thank the customer for bringing the issue to your attention and sincerely mean it. Remember that only a few customers care enough to complain to you, the majority simply walk away and take their business to the competition. Service consultant Marylin Suttle puts it this way:

"Thank your customer for complaining and mean it. Most will never bother to complain. They will just walk away."

Then apologize gracefully to the customer without necessarily admitting liability. A general apology will do for most customers. You could say something like:

Mr. Patrick, sorry for what has happened, this is quite unfortunate. Let me see what I can do about it, Mr. Patrick, and I will call you back shortly.

Or

Madam Jane kindly accept my apology for this delay, let me find out what happened and get back to you in thirty minutes, we are truly sorry Madam Jane.

vi. Find a solution

You have now understood the customer's problem and have offered your empathy and apology, now it's time to take action to correct the mistake. Find the most appropriate solution to the issue at hand and give the customer realistic timelines. It is in your interest to clearly explain to the customer the steps you will take to solve the problem.

You could say things like:

Mr. Patrick, I have checked our system and I can see that your loan facility is at the approval stage. I will call the concerned staff right away to fast-track the approval. I will let you know the outcome of the approval by afternoon today; I will then have a colleague of mine at the head office to take your file to the disbursement desk in case of a positive verdict. We expect to close this issue by tomorrow at 10.00 a.m., is that ok with you Mr. Patrick?

Or

Madam Jane, the reference number in your order sheet indicates that your payment was received on Wednesday last week; let me call the warehouse immediately to find out why the delivery was not done, I will ensure that your materials are delivered to your site this afternoon Madam Jane. I have confirmed with the lo-

gistics manager that there is available truck that shall use that same route to do other deliveries. I surely hope this will be ok with you Madam Jane; once again, accept my sincere apology.

For customer service sake, prioritize these cases that have been brought to your attention. In as much as it is within your power, make it up to them. There are very many inexpensive ways to make up for such service slip-ups. Going a little extra expense for the sake of the customer will go a long way in saving the client relationship and loss of business.

Dealing with angry customers

> *"Your most unhappy customers are your greatest source of learning"* ~ Bill Gates

What about those customers who are pissed off and plainly angry? How do you handle them and ensure a win-win situation? The approach is similar in principle to what we have discussed above. Stay calm and resist the urge to talk back to them in an aggressive manner. We encourage the approach of the **HEAT** technique.

HEAT is an acronym which stands for:

- *Hear them out*
- *Empathize*
- *Acknowledge your fault and apologize*
- *Take action*

Kindly note:

✓ Recognize that the customer is distressed and thus is display-

ing that kind of aggression.
- ✓ Let the customer vent it out.
- ✓ Don't take it personally.
- ✓ Probe them calmly by asking them open ended questions to know more about the problem.
- ✓ Since such incidents can create a commotion, beware that other customers could be watching.
- ✓ Listen more and speak less.
- ✓ Relate with their situation by being empathetic.
- ✓ Respectfully address them by their names.
- ✓ Gracefully acknowledge your fault and apologize as appropriate.
- ✓ Know when to give in.
- ✓ Let them know you appreciate their feedback and continued patronage.
- ✓ Find solution to their issues and prioritize the same.
- ✓ Explain to them the steps you will take to solve their problem.
- ✓ Remain courteous.
- ✓ Your voice should show that you care.

Dealing with rude or abusive customers

- ✓ Hear them out out—encourage the customers to talk, the more they vent out, the less aggressive they become.
- ✓ Show understanding of the problem.
- ✓ Don't take it personally.
- ✓ Let them calmly know that the kind of language they are using is not acceptable, and that it will not help to solve the problem at hand.
- ✓ Empathize with their situation.
- ✓ If you cannot calm them down, arrange for a break. You could say that you will call them back after checking up the reference number, or that you are going to fetch a particular document.

Dealing with a non-responsive customer

- ✓ Let the customer know what you are going to do during the call or after you have finished speaking to them. This will put them more at ease as they can see the next course of action.
- ✓ Ask open questions and respond favorably with your answers.
- ✓ Do also frequently ask closed questions to see if the customer is till with you.

Dealing with an emotional customer

- ✓ First and foremost, listen actively.
- ✓ Don't take it personally.
- ✓ Ask probing questions to uncover the reality of the situation.
- ✓ Build rapport with the customer through empathy.
- ✓ Don't get caught up in their emotion.
- ✓ Calmly restate the problem as the customer sees it and the feelings associated with it.
- ✓ Let them know you agree with their right to have such feelings—you could say things like: *You are right to be upset about this, Mr. Patrick*
- ✓ Ask the 'how' questions to get the person to the problem solving mode.
- ✓ Move to action plan as soon as you can.
- ✓ Whatever happens, try as much as possible to manage the outcome and not the emotion.

When dealing with all the challenging customers, always keep in mind the following:

- You are dealing with a fellow human being who has feelings.
- Use the customer's name when talking with them.
- Respond as if all your customers are watching.
- Never attempt to match the aggression of your custom-

ers. Don't answer fire with fire.

- Listen to understand and not to answer back.

Reflection questions:

1) What is your experience with handling challenging customers?
2) Active listening to the customers has been touted as a valuable tip in handling challenging customers, in what practical ways can you foster this technique?
3) Your most unhappy customers are your greatest source of learning; to what extent do you agree or disagree with this statement? Please elaborate.
4) Why do you think it is helpful to call customers by their names when talking to them?
5) What other tips could you use to successfully navigate the conversation with an angry or disappointed customer to arrive at a win-win scenario?

CHAPTER TEN: SOME NUGGETS OF SERVICE EXCELLENCE

Building a good reputation in business definitely takes time but the results though gradual will be worth it. Indeed the path to excellence might seem difficult at first, but by taking small regular steps you eventually make very significant progress. It will however require patience, persistence and most importantly, a strong will to push it through.

In your pursuit of service excellence, the following tips will help to set your company apart from the crowd.

1. Things to do religiously:

- ✓ *Think long term*
- ✓ *Get close to and know your customers*
- ✓ *Know and befriend the Key Decision Makers*
- ✓ *Be available for your customers*
- ✓ *Be proactive*
- ✓ *Practice continuous improvement*
- ✓ *Go the extra mile*

Let's elaborate the above points hereunder:

a) Think long term

> *"If you make a sale, you can make a living. If you make an investment of time and good service, you can make a fortune" ~ Jim Rohm*

A customer is for life. Your decisions and actions concerning customer service should be done with longevity in perspective. Avoid making hasty decisions in the heat of the moment without considering the ramifications thereof. Your greatest concern should not be the immediate closure of the transaction at hand but rather the building of an ongoing business relationship.

It pays handsome dividends to approach the management of every customer relationship with the lenses of **Customer Lifetime Value (CLV).**

b) Get close to and know your customers

> *"Get closer to your customers, so close that you tell them what they need before they know it themselves" ~ Steve Jobs*

It is about being realistic or pragmatic. Realism requires that you have a correct view of the world outside your business to be prepared to adapt to its reality and make rational judgment about the threats that are fundamental to the survival of your business and which ones will cost you more to fight than you could possibly win.

If you are in the financial services sector or any other service sector for that matter, do spend more time in the field than in the office. The rule of thumb is to spend at least **60%** of your working hours with your customers in the field and only about **40%** of your working time in the office. This helps you to gather ground level intelligence by being out there observing consumer behavior in the market place, as opposed to just receiving reports.

Being close to your customers allows you to understand more and to accurately diagnose and make appropriate prescriptions to the customers' problems even before they themselves become aware of the same.

c) Know and befriend the Key Decision Makers

In every business, there is always the critical team of the decision makers, this team is known as the **Decision Making Unit** (DMU). As a relationship manager, get to know the members of this critical team. The members of this team could include the personal secretary to the Managing Director, the finance manager, or the chief operations officer (COO). They are basically the people who have the ears of the Chief Executive Officer.

The members of the DMU are the real power brokers in any company. They are the ones who decide whether their firm shall continue being your customer, or when your payments shall be made in case of a debtor-creditor business relationship.

Visit and befriend the DMU members more often and occasionally carry some give-away(s). There are always some inexpensive presents you could consider such as branded company merchandise like diaries and notebooks.

Occasionally treating your key customers to a surprise lunch will communicate in kind that you really value their business relationship. In the Bible, the LORD Jesus admonished His listeners to make friends using the unrighteous mammon (**Luke 16:9**).

Kindly note that the use of phone calls and letters alone do not work very well in long term business relationships; on the contrary, regular visits do. You could also consider organizing occasional luncheons and dinners for your key customers, where you could invite some resource persons to do talks on business related topics.

d) Be available for your customers

> *"When a customer comes first, a customer will last" ~ Robert Half*

In your day to day operations you might become very busy and forget who your real bosses are—the customers. Purpose to be available for your customers on a priority basis; this book advises that you should have a predictable day schedule and plan for the time when you can be seen by your clients.

Remember to receive your customers' calls—don't be known as the manager who is always too busy for his clients, too busy even to receive their calls.

It actually beats logic how someone chooses to ignore his or her customers' calls when the customers are their actual employers. Imagine for a minute what would happen if you are a junior staff in an organization and you ignore the calls from your CEO or the HR Manager, and repeatedly do so! Well, in reality that's what happens when you ignore your customers' calls. You eventually get fired by them.

Needless to say that you will also need your customers to receive your phone calls when it comes to it.

e) Be proactive

It is not enough to just react to problems if you want to be a cut above the rest. Taking own initiative and contacting your customers when a problem arises before they have a chance to reach out to you shows that you are prioritizing the issue at hand and you are acting with urgency and understanding. This type of vigilance is what separates a great service organization from the rest.

Anticipate your customers' issues and prepare to give them solutions ahead of time. Don't be caught off-guard by your customers when they are making queries and asking for particular line of information or service.

f)   Practice continuous improvement

"Perfection is not attainable, but if we chase perfection, we can catch excellence" ~ Vince Lombardi

The biggest room in the world is the room for improvement. Always strive to become better than you were yesterday. Always make use of customer feedback to improve your service offering —it's also the best available way to understand your customers' sentiments and to know whether or not your efforts are paying dividends.

There are so many reporting and analytics tools at your disposal, you can use the same to get a clear picture of what's working and what's not. This way you can plug the gaps in your customer service support and keep improving your customers' experience as a result.

g)   Go the extra mile

"There are no traffic jams along the extra mile" ~ Rauger Staubach

In offering service excellence, always strive to do more than is required of you—go the extra mile. Going the extra mile is what exceeds the customers' expectations and puts a smile on their faces –it is what *wows* the customers. Going the extra mile for your customers is what creates the emotional bond with the customers and wins their loyalty.

In this era of cutthroat competition, doing only what is expected of you or serving by the book shall not set you apart from the pack.

You can be the pace setter in your industry by simply going the extra mile and offering pleasant surprises to your customers. Let the other players labour to catch up with you. Just like the NFL hall of famer Rauger Staubach observed, there are no traffic jams along the extra mile; there the journey is smoother, faster and fuel-saving.

2. **And then there is some more, always remember the following:**
   - *Remain professional*
   - *Keep client confidentiality*
   - *Say no with dignity*
   - *Fix things when they go wrong*
   - *Use the 80-20 rule*

We shall elaborate the same hereunder:

a. Remain professional

In your zeal to impress and embrace your customers, kindly know the boundaries. Keep your interactions with your customers very professional and they will respect you for it. Never divulge sensitive company secrets to your customers.

Don't paint your seniors and other colleagues' in negative light in front of your customers; equally don't talk negatively about your competitors and business rivals before your customers.

Even more importantly, as relationship manager don't engage in personal business with your customers. This potentially creates conflicts of interests and clouds objectivity in judgment. Engaging in personal businesses with your customers has the potential of jeopardizing your current relationship with your customers.

b. Keep client confidentiality

> *To whom much is given, much is expected (Luke 12:48)*

In your daily interaction with your customers, you will learn both business and personal information about your customers; keep this information strictly confidential unless they have expressly given their consent to publicize it. Customers will also look up to you for advice on a wide range of issues that may go beyond the business at hand, do you best to keep their trust.

Remember to whom much is given, much is expected (**Luke 12:48**)

c. Learn to say no with dignity

> *"The customer may not always be right, but they are always the customer. So, let the customer be wrong with dignity and respect"*
> *~Shep Hyken*

Your customer will occasionally be wrong or fail to live up to their side of the bargain, do let them be wrong with dignity. Remember that you are dealing with a person not just data. Your **no** should be made clear that it is a no to the idea or the issue at hand only and not a rejection of the customer as a person.

Learn to say no with dignity and give your customers hope. They may not qualify for the product or the service they are currently seeking but with your proper advice, they could surely qualify for the same tomorrow. Don't be a dream killer.

The late American civil rights activist, poet, singer and best-selling author Maya Angelou, said that:

> *"People will forget what you said, people will forget what you did, but people will never forget how you made them feel."*

d. Fix things when they go wrong

> *"Customers don't expect you to be perfect; they do expect you to fix things when they go wrong"*
> *~Donald Porter*

In the course of business, some things will definitely not go as planned and thereby result into customer disservice. When things go wrong, become proactive and fix them. Customers do not expect perfection all the time, but they definitely expect you to fix the arising issues. When they complain to you, do your best to right the wrongs in a speedy or timely manner.

e. 80-20 Rule

In every business, it has been noted that only about **20%** of the customers actually command about **80%** of the business portfolio. It pays huge dividends to invest in closer working relationship with this group of customers. Make deliberate effort to know these customers. Let them know you care and value them as persons, beyond the business they bring to you.

Know and participate as much as possible in their key events such as the birthdays for their children, their anniversaries, their bereavements etc. In other words be there for these customers in both their high and low moments.

Reflection questions:

1) Getting to know your customers requires that you spend more time with them, how would you implement this strategy if you are not doing the same already?

2) In what inexpensive ways could you use to build rapport with your key customers and members of the DMUs of your corporate customers?

3) Customer feedback is a great resource for gauging your level of service offering, in what ways does your brand use the customer feedback to improve on the customer experience?

4) Going the extra mile is what wows the customers, in what practical ways can your brand actualize this strategy in the day-to-day customer service offering?

5) In the list of things to always keep in mind discussed in this chapter, in which area(s) are you or your company most deficient? How would you address the gap(s)?

CHAPTER ELEVEN: COMMUNICATION IN BUSINESS

"Cash flowing into your business is in direct proportion to the communication flowing out."

~ AUTHOR UNKNOWN

In business, no skill is more important than the ability to communicate effectively. This is especially vital in customer service, where communication can make or break business relationships.

Communication is usually more complex than it is normally perceived. Within the communication process, two or more people attempt to arrive at shared meaning and understanding. For this process to be effective, both the sender and the receiver must engage in both talking and listening.

Every business person should know and master effective communication skills. These include public speaking, written correspondence and non-verbal communication. Warren Buffet, the

American billionaire business mogul, investor and philanthropist avers that having all the brain power in the world without knowing how to communicate will not give you success. He equates lack of good communication skills—both oral and written to *winking at a girl in the dark*. He said:

"If you can't communicate, it's like winking at a girl in the dark, nothing happens." ~Warren Buffet.[15]

Your effectiveness in communication or lack of it thereof has a direct impact on your success or otherwise in the business. Effective communication is what nurtures the much needed positive relationship with the various key stakeholders of the business. The better at communicating you are, and the more people you communicate with, the better your cash flow will be. On the other hand, when you are poor at communication, your business invariably suffers a great deal; and your cash flow gets negatively impacted as a result.

Service excellence demands that you need to communicate with your customers more frequently, right from their on-boarding and throughout the life of the business relationship. For example, let your customers clearly understand the terms and conditions of the product and service contracts; do also communicate promptly with your customers on any changes in the company policies and product offering. Mass communication is good but personalized one-on-one engagement is preferred especially with your key customers.

The other side of communication is equally vital, that of listening to your customers. ***Listen to your customers to understand and not just to reply.*** For good customer service sake, get into the habit of actively listening, your primary goal should be to understand your customers' needs and expectations. Take time to appreciate your customers' feedback and use that feedback to improve on their experience with your brand.

Give prompt feedback on the customers' queries and applications. Where there are delays beyond your control, inform the customers accordingly and keep them posted on any progress made; always give your customers realistic expectations, if possible do under-promise and over-deliver—this will give a *wow* experience.

In case you are in creditor-debtor relationship with your customers, kindly ensure that during debt follow up you document your correspondences and keep copies in a safe place for future reference. Have the customers make their commitments to honor their payment promises in writing. Mind your language and conduct during any debt follow up engagement with the customers.

Service Excellence Influences Customers' Communication About A Brand

One of the most powerful forms of communication that affects a business is one over which you have little or no control: the communication from your existing customers to your potential customers. You can however influence the trajectory of this realm of communication by simply focusing on what you can control—*offering service excellence.*

Superior customer service will earn you an army of volunteer advocates freely broadcasting how incredible it is to do business with you. The power of this word-of-mouth advertising is immeasurable. ***Your loyal customers turned fans will always prove to be a social premium, a buffer of defense in case of a service slip-up.***

On the other hand, treating your customers with indifference and lethargy is sure to ferment negative publicity from the angry and dissatisfied customers. Viral negative publicity from angry and disappointed customers is a proven path to business oblivion.

For this reason, effective communication is a vital function for any company. *Having a communications department is great, but the real communication normally happens in the day-to-day interactions between your customer-facing-staff and your customers.* This communication is in the attitude displayed by your employees, their body language, the tone and words they use, and ultimately in the actions and inactions of your staff every day. It is therefore imperative that you adequately train your employees on the ABCs of communication, the business language and cordial relationship building skills with the customers.

Kindly take note that *effective communication is a skill that can be learned and mastered,* you can therefore purpose to have your team trained in this important business skill, and see your business relationships greatly enhanced. Investment in effective communication skills invariably results into improved bottom line.

Reflection questions:

1) Communication is a key parameter in the success or otherwise of every business, in what ways can your brand harness the power of communication to ensure business success?

2) In what practical ways can your business brand influence the trajectory of the communication from your existing customers to your potential customers?

3) The real communication happens in the day-to-day interactions between your customer-facing-staff and your customers. How can your company ensure that this communication is aiding the achievement of the company mission and vision, as opposed to actively vetoing the same?

THE END

BIBLIOGRAPHY:

1. Customer Experience Management: Engaging loyal customers to evangelize your brand *Aberdeen Group Report*, 2018

2. State of Customer Service Survey 2019: Research report *Hubspot,* page 22 at https://blog.hubspot.com/service/customer-service-2019 accessed on June 4, 2020

3. Infographics at https://www.business2community.com/customer-experience/stop-losing-money-focus-customer-service-infographic-0663834/amp accessed on May 6, 2020

4. Ron Kaufman, *Uplifting Service: The Proven Path to Delighting Your Customers, Colleagues, and Everyone else You Meet* (Evolve Publishing, 2012) Page xxiii

5. State of customer service survey 2019: Research report by *Hubspot,* page 19 at https://blog.hubspot.com/service/customer-service-2019 accessed on June 4, 2020

6. What customers want at https://www.forbes.com/sites/shephyken/2019/05/05/what-your-customers-really-want/#30c8dbde54fd accessed on June 7, 2020

7. Pursuit of Excellence by Vala Afshar at https://www.salesforce.com/blog/2017/01/data-the-connected-customers-wants.html accessed on June 4, 2020

8. Infographics at https://www.business2community.com/customer-experience/stop-losing-money-focus-customer-

service-infographic-0663834/amp accessed on May 6, 2020

9. Deviney E David (1998) *Outstanding Customer Service: The Key to Customer Loyalty*, (Coastal Training Technologies Corp) page.16

10. Customer experience maturity monitor (2009), by *Peppers & Rodgers group*

11. Infographics at https://www.business2community.com/customer-experience/stop-losing-money-focus-customer-service-infographic-0663834/amp accessed on May 6, 2020

12. Infographics at https://www.business2community.com/customer-experience/stop-losing-money-focus-customer-service-infographic-0663834/amp accessed on May 6, 2020

13. Customer satisfaction at https://www.briantracy.com/blog/business-success/rules-of-customer-satisfaction-customer-loyalty/ accessed on May 6, 2020

14. Peter Shankman tweet at https://twitter.com/petershankman/status/103936299983060993

15. Warren Buffet: How to increase your worth at https://www.cnbc.com accessed on March 5, 2019

AFTERWORD

The power of service excellence in the building of formidable business brands is enormous. Nothing can take the sacred place of service excellence in delivering sustainable business success. This is because business success or lack of it thereof ultimately comes down to the level of customers' patronage. Without the customers there is no business, end of discussion.

Service excellence is perhaps the only magical thing that sets insanely successful business brands apart from the mediocre majority that cannot be readily copied by the competition. In this book, we have labored to put forward the essential tenets of service excellence in one cover for the benefit of the business leaders, management teams and customer service representatives.

Attaining service excellence is a marathon journey that requires patience, persistence and passion on the part of the organizational leadership; it is not a sprint or overnight phenomenon. We are however persuaded that the returns on investment in the improvement of customer service standards far outweigh any costs and disruptive inconveniences that may be incurred along the way. Leading companies understand this pay off very well and are therefore perpetually devoted to the never ending journey of improving their service standards.

We trust that you have noted from this book that far from being helpless in the face of growing cutthroat competition with commoditized products and services, in an environment rife with new risks and increased government oversight, you actually have the power and the wherewithal within your control to victoriously navigate through all these forces and emerge as a formidable player with super profitability to boot, in your specific industry. The secret lies in embracing service excellence.

We believe that the information contained herein has been both useful and helpful to the readers. You can take the right steps and build a culture of service excellence within your establishment and reap the immense benefits that come with it. Your customers are waiting.

Possibly you may need help or support in training your organization on service excellence or you may require more information on the aforementioned issues. We would like to hear from you. You can contact us on any of the below listed avenues and we will be both delighted and honored to partner with you on your journey of turning around your business into a formidable brand.

We are a team of experts drawn from various professions that work together to assist clients to unlock their full potential for growth and profitability, hence achieving greatness and prestige that comes with it. We do this through our consultancy firm— **Hezma Ventures Consulting.**

About Hezma Ventures Consulting

Hezma Ventures Consulting is a premier leadership development and business management consultancy firm based in Kenya.

Our Purpose

We exist to empower individuals and organizations to significantly increase their performance capacity in order to achieve worthwhile purposes in life

Our Mission

We work with leaders and teams to create powerful cultures of excellence that spur peak performances while having fun in the process. We do this through training programs that captures the hearts and minds of staff members of our clients and align them with the company purpose. This results in having highly engaged teams that are both proactive and highly productive; thus reducing costs of operations and delivering premium returns to the client companies.

Our Vision

To become a world class consulting powerhouse positively contributing to the development and prosperity of individuals and organizations

Our contact information

You can contact us through any of the following:

Postal address: P.O Box 2262-50200 Bungoma, Kenya
E-mail: info@hezmaventures.co.ke; willis.amach@gmail.com
Telephone: +254 723 440 148/ +254 724 572 472
WhatsApp: +254 723 440 148

Facebook page: Hezma Ventures

ACKNOWLEDGEMENT

Many persons have been instrumental in my personal growth and development, for want of space I will mention only a few people.

To start with I'm grateful to God the Almighty who is the source of life and all good gifts; my life today is a testimony of God's faithfulness.

Special appreciation goes to my dear wife Christine –the love of my life and companion in this life journey. Your patience and understanding has afforded me the time and space to write this book. You are the best thing to have happened to me after my encounter with the LORD Jesus.

I would like to mention some special people whose impact in my career has had a huge influence on my world view and appreciation of the noble place of service excellence in the corporate world: Elizabeth Gathai—the long serving Director of Credit at Equity Bank Group, you were my first trainer on service excellence and career growth, your passion for service excellence is in its own class; Eric Tuda—the Business Growth and Development Manager at Equity Bank ltd and my immediate supervisor, your passion for service excellence and ability to appreciate and inspire your subordinates to career excellence is incredible; Jacqueline Nyaga—the long serving Head of Talent Management at UAP-Old Mutual Group and currently practicing HR Consultant and Leadership Coach, your energy and passion to bring out the best out of your staff is extra ordinary.

I would also like to thank my customers both individuals and corporates who gave me an opportunity to partner with them in their pursuit of excellence, career growth and personal development. Your valuable feedback has been pivotal in enriching our services. Space would not afford me the opportunity to mention all of you by names; the omission is not out of spite. Thank you very much.

The Author

ABOUT THE AUTHOR

Willis Amach

 Willis Amach is a minister of the Word of God, Corporate trainer, Management and Leadership Consultant and Service Excellence Enthusiast. He is a Kenyatta University—School of Business Alumnus, where he graduated with Honors in Bachelor of Commerce-Accounting Option. He is also an alumnus of Daystar University, Institute of Leadership and Professional Development (ILPD) and a Certified Public Accountant (CPA).

He is a former career banker having served in various capacities including management positions with local banks for a period of twelve years, before resigning voluntarily to pursue his calling in ministry and other personal interests. He has authored other books such as: Experiencing Victorious Kingdom Life Now—Victory to Victory Every Day, Make Super Profits in any Economy—Master the Seven Secrets of the Super Brands, Break Through the Barriers—Shatter Your Limitations and Business Success Beyond Profit—Building a Corporate Culture of Excellence.

Willis is married to one wife Christine, and they live together in Bungoma County, Kenya.

BOOKS BY THIS AUTHOR

Experiencing Victorious Kingdom Life Now

The subject of the Kingdom of God is primarily the message of the gospel. The Gospel is about the King of Kings and His coming Kingdom. This was the core message of the LORD Jesus Christ. Though lost to the contemporary Christian, it is at the gospel that the apostles of the early Church preached.

This book seeks to reintroduce this lost gem to the hurting and disillusioned world with a waning Christian Influence. We trace this concept from the very beginning of time, to when and how it was lost and how to rediscover and appropriate its full benefits here and now on account of what Jesus Christ has done on the cross, as we await with the blessed hope for the glorious appearance of our LORD and Savior Jesus Christ in the fullness of time.

Make Super Profits In Any Economy

In the business world, there are countless businesses today comprising of many struggling entities, a few stable ventures and an even smaller number of insanely successful enterprises spread across all industries and business sectors.

These latter brands have achieved market distinctions by being truly differentiated from their competitors. They have become well known for consistently offering high quality products and superior services; they can be relied upon to deliver consistently on their promises.

As these titans seem to have it all easy, "taking all the customers" and making all the money, for the rest of the businesses, it seems to be all struggles just to get by with very little or nothing to show for their efforts.

We have established that these super brands have certain secrets or pillars in common that ensure their success no matter the prevailing economic circumstances. The collective and faithful application of these secrets enable these businesses to build and sustain well-oiled product and service delivery machineries to a growing pool of satisfied and happy customers, with an exactness that can be replicated.

In this book, the author unveisl these secrets in one cover for the benefit of the business leaders and all budding entrepreneurs.

Now you too can purpose to join this elite league of the super achievers by utilizing these secrets or pillars in your business, and stand to enjoy the immense rewards that come with it.

Break Through The Barriers

Every person at one time or another has had dreams of doing something great with their lives, but not many people have mastered the courage to pursue those dreams. Many people continue to live in very deprived conditions despite the enormous potential and God-given capabilities packaged within them; they just do enough to get by and possibly arrive safely at the graveyard.

The few that make positive impact in this world and live their lives to the fullest, those who master the courage to do what the rest are afraid to do, are the ones who have developed their inner persons to the point of breaking through the life and environmental barriers and shattered the limitations imposed upon them by personal deficiencies, culture and traditions.

We aver that success is not for the chosen few, rather it is for the few who choose. You too can purpose to break through your barriers and live your life to the fullest, making positive impact and leaving the world a better place. In this book we show you how...